Student Workbook

Grade K

Scott Foresman

Editorial Offices: Glenview, Illinois • Parsippany, New Jersey • New York, New York
Sales Offices: Parsippany, New Jersey • Duluth, Georgia • Glenview, Illinois
Carrollton, Texas • Ontario, California

www.sfscience.com

Series Authors

Dr. Timothy Cooney
Professor of Earth Science and Science Education
Earth Science Department
University of Northern Iowa
Cedar Falls, Iowa

Michael Anthony DiSpezio
Science Education Specialist
Cape Cod Children's Museum
Falmouth, Massachusetts

Barbara K. Foots
Science Education Consultant
Houston, Texas

Dr. Angie L. Matamoros
Science Curriculum Specialist
Broward County Schools
Ft. Lauderdale, Florida

Kate Boehm Nyquist
Science Writer and Curriculum Specialist
Mount Pleasant, South Carolina

Dr. Karen L. Ostlund
Professor
Science Education Center
The University of Texas at Austin
Austin, Texas

Contributing Authors

Dr. Anna Uhl Chamot
Associate Professor and ESL Faculty Advisor
Department of Teacher Preparation and Special Education
Graduate School of Education and Human Development
The George Washington University
Washington, D.C.

Dr. Jim Cummins
Professor
Modern Language Centre and Curriculum Development
Ontario Institute for Studies in Education
Toronto, Canada

Gale Phillips Kahn
Lecturer, Science and Math Education
Elementary Education Department
California State University, Fullerton
Fullerton, California

Vince Sipkovich
Teacher
Irvine United School District
Irvine, California

Steve Weinberg
Science Consultant
Connecticut State Department of Education
Hartford, Connecticut

ISBN: 0-328-03420-7

8 9 0 - VO39 - 06 05 04

Contents

	Page Numbers	Use with TE Pages
Unit A • Life Science		
Chapter 1: Living and Nonliving	**1-9**	A5-A9a
Chapter 2: Animals	**11-23**	A13-A19a
Chapter 3: Plants	**25-39**	A23-A31a
Unit B • Physical Science		
Chapter 1: Matter	**41-53**	B5-B11a
Chapter 2: Sound, Heat, and Light	**55-69**	B15-B23
Chapter 3: Movement	**71-83**	B27-B33a
Unit C • Earth Science		
Chapter 1: Earth and Sky	**85-97**	C5-C11a
Chapter 2: Weather	**99-107**	C15-C19a
Chapter 3: Caring for Earth	**109-123**	C23-C31a
Unit D • Human Body		
Chapter 1: Your Senses	**125-137**	D5-D11a
Chapter 2: Growing and Changing	**139-151**	D15-D21a
Chapter 3: Being Healthy	**153-167**	D25-D33a
My Process Skills		
Observing	**3-4**	2-3
Communicating	**5-6**	4-5
Classifying	**7-8**	6-7
Estimating and Measuring	**9-10**	8-9
Inferring	**11-12**	10-11
Predicting	**13-14**	12-13
Making Definitions	**15-16**	14-15
Making and Using Models	**17-18**	16-17
Giving Hypothesis	**19-20**	18-19
Collecting Data	**21-22**	20-21
Controlling Variables	**23-24**	22-23
Experimenting	**25-26**	24-25

Name ____________________

Family Activity
Unit A Chapter 1

Dear Family,

Our class will be learning about living things and nonliving things. We will learn to identify living things such as plants and animals and nonliving things such as toys and rocks.

In the space, I drew a picture that shows living and nonliving things. On the back of this page are ideas for activities that you and I can do together to get started learning about living and nonliving things.

Name ________________________________

Science at Home

Here are some activities we can do together.

Guessing Game

I'll look around the room and find a living thing.
You ask me questions until you guess it.
Then you find a nonliving thing.
I'll ask you questions to guess it.

Label It

First we'll cut a sheet of paper into four pieces.
Next we'll write yes or no on each piece.
Then I'll put the yes labels on some living things.
Last I'll put the no labels on some nonliving things.

Science in the Community

Help your child "adopt" a living thing found in your neighborhood such as a garden or sidewalk plant. Assist your child in caring for this living thing for several days. During this period, encourage your child to observe and draw pictures of this living thing. Talk about how your child is helping this living thing to meet some of its needs.

Name ______________________________

Living Things I Saw

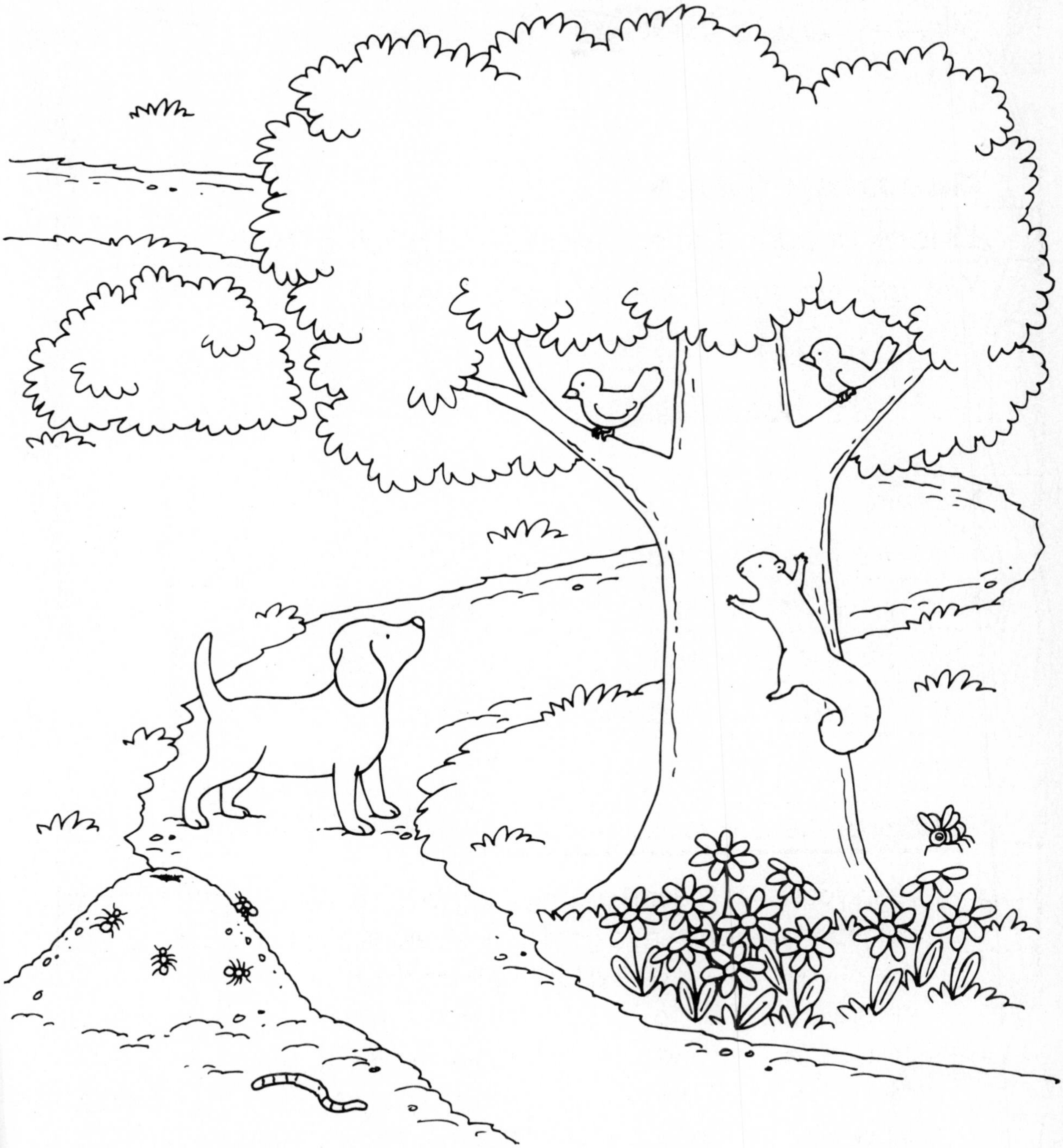

Notes for Home Your child colored pictures showing living things.
Home Activity: Ask your child to point to a living thing and tell something about it.

Name ______________________________________

What Living Things Need

Notes for Home Your child found a picture of a living thing and drew something that this living thing needs.
Home Activity: Ask your child how he or she might help a plant get what it needs.

Name ____________________

Explore Activity
Unit A Chapter 1

Explore growing sprouts.

Draw.

1

2

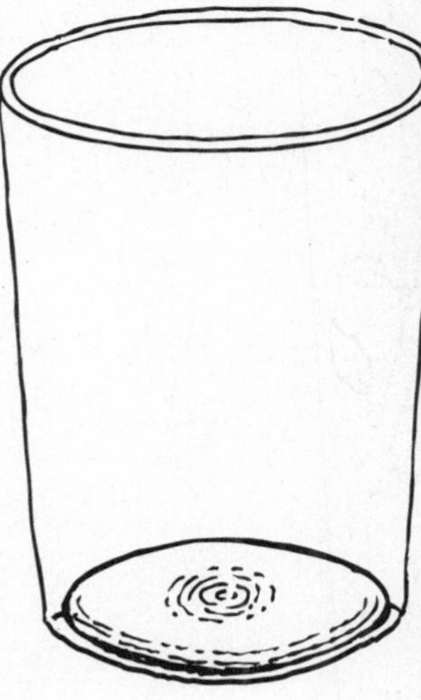

3

4

5

6

Notes for Home Your child drew pictures to show what happens over time to alfalfa seeds that are kept moist.
Home Activity: Use the pictures to talk with your child about how the seeds changed over time.

Name ______________________________

Explore Activity
Unit A Chapter 1

Nonliving Things in a Home

What nonliving things are in a home?

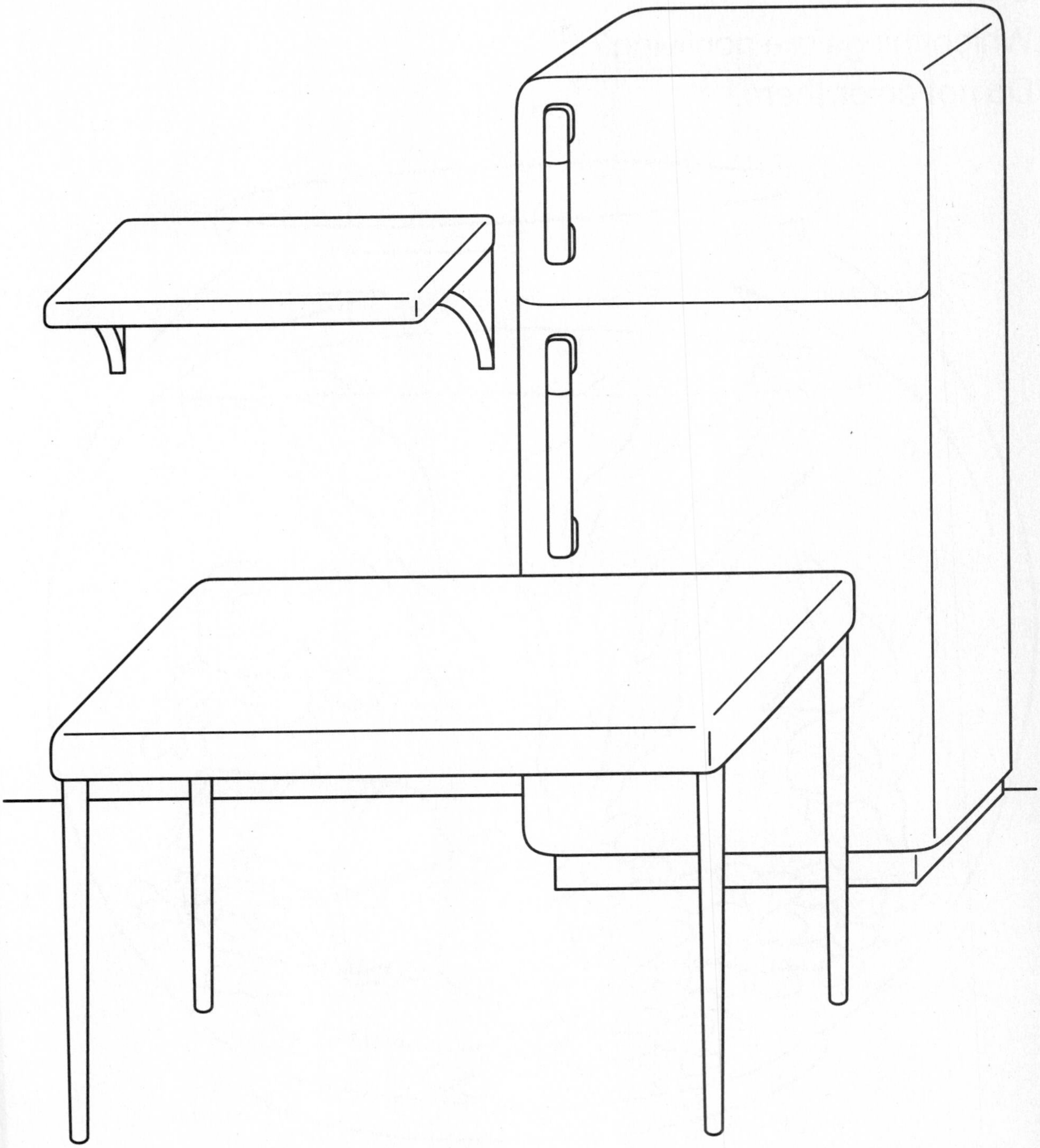

Notes for Home Your child drew some nonliving things that could be found in a home.
Home Activity: Ask your child to point to a nonliving thing in your home and tell something about it.

Name ______________________________

Explore Activity
Unit A Chapter 1

Living or Nonliving?

Which things are living?
Color them.
Which things are nonliving?
Do not color them.

Notes for Home Your child colored the living things in this fishbowl.
Home Activity: Ask your child how he or she might care for the living things in this fishbowl.

Name ______________________________

Explore Activity
Unit A Chapter 1

Explore living and nonliving objects.

Draw.

Living	Nonliving

Notes for Home Your child drew pictures to show living and nonliving objects found in a soil sample.
Home Activity: As you walk outside with your child, point to objects and have your child tell if they are living or nonliving.

Name

Family Activity
Unit A Chapter 2

Dear Family,
Our class will be learning about animals, what animals need, and animal babies. In the space, I drew a picture of an animal I know or like. On the back of this page are some ideas of things we can do together to learn about animals.

Name ____________________

Science at Home

Here are some games we can play:

"Animal Riddles"

First listen to these clues.
This animal has
soft fur,
long ears,
and hops.
What is it?

Now you give me a clue.

"Animal Pictionary"

First draw a picture of an animal.
I'll tell you what it is.
Then I'll draw a picture.
You tell me what animal it is.

Science in the Community

When you're out and about with your child, become animal watchers. Observe coverings, movement, and animal interaction. Keep a log of drawings and any interesting facts you and your child learn from your observations.

Name ______________________________

Explore Activity
Unit A Chapter 2

How Do Animals Move?

Frogs **hop.**

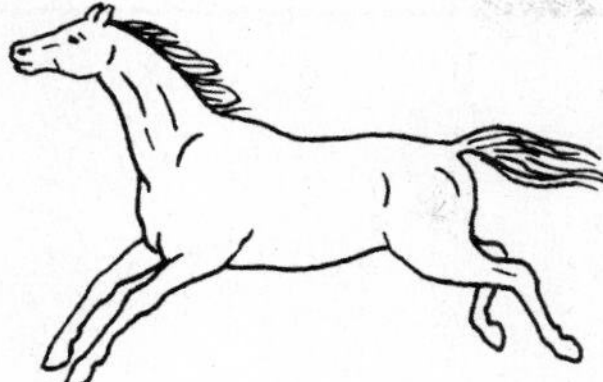

Horses **run.**

Pigs **walk.**

Birds **fly.**

Fish **swim.**

Snakes **crawl.**

walk	fly
swim	crawl

Notes for Home Your child drew pictures of animals that move in different ways.
Home Activity: Have your child move like an animal while you guess what the animal is.

Name ______________________________

Animal Coverings

 fur
 feathers
 scales
 smooth skin
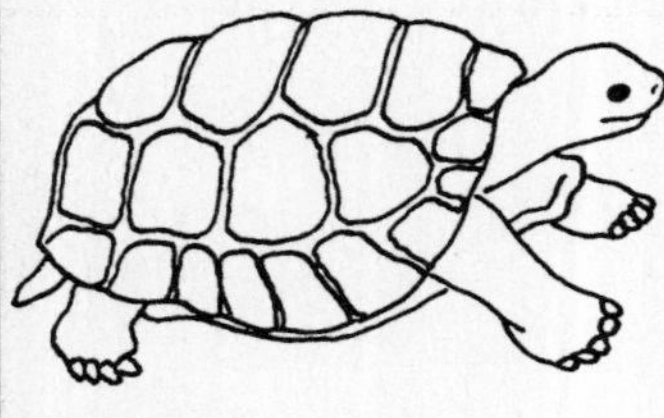 shell

Notes for Home Your child drew or pasted pictures to show animals with different body coverings.
Home Activity: Ask your child to tell you about each body covering and how it helps the animal.

Name ________________

Explore Activity
Unit A Chapter 2

Explore feathers.

Trial	(feather)	(downy feather)
1		
2		
3		
4		
5		

Notes for Home Your child made tally marks to show which feather stayed airborne longer for each trial. ***Home Activity:*** Look outside for birds with your child. Observe and discuss how the feathers look when the birds are flying and when they are resting.

Name ______________________

Bird Watch

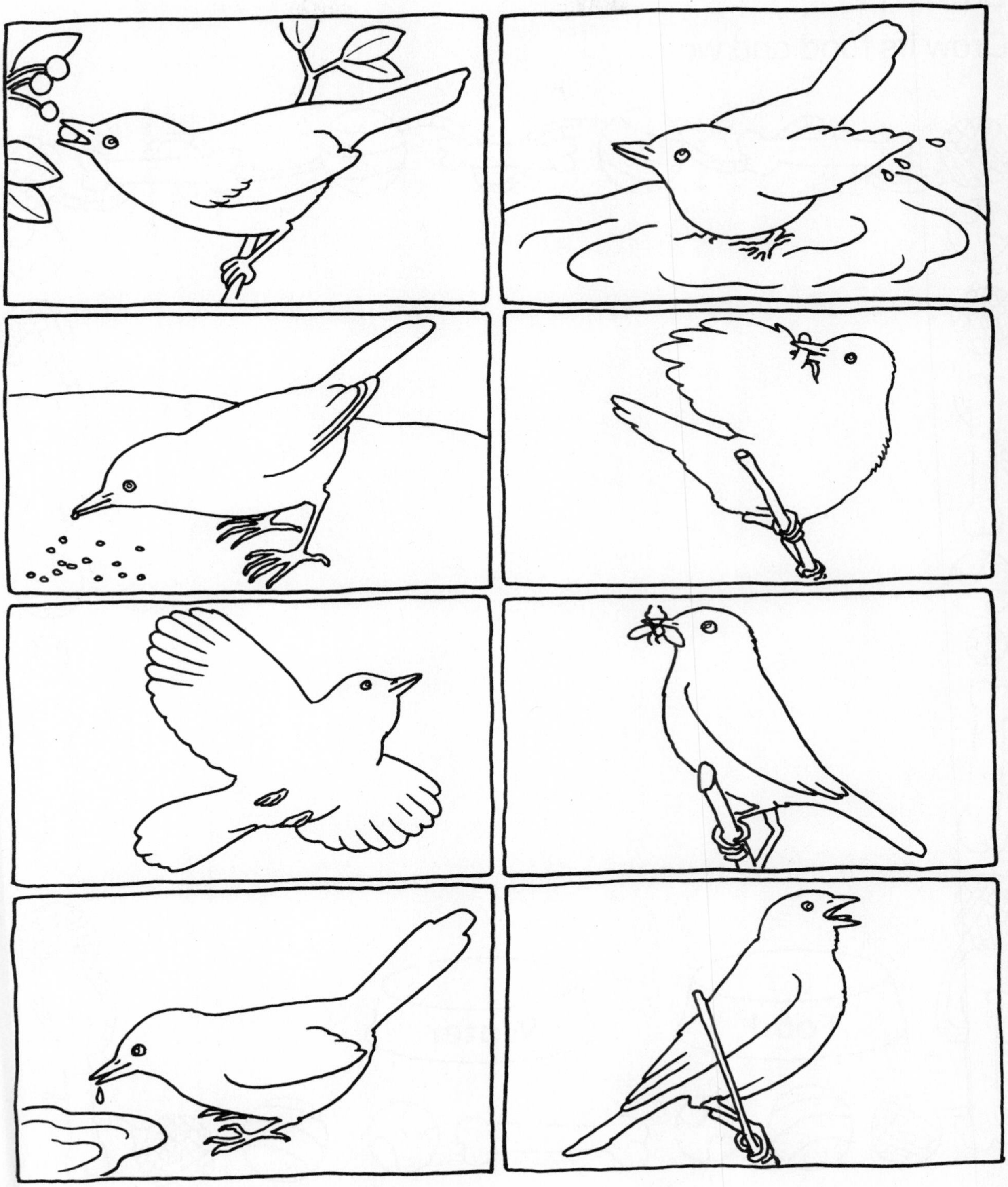

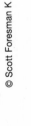

Notes for Home Your child observed birds and colored to show what he or she observed.
Home Activity: You and your child can look for examples of different bird behavior near your home and talk about what you see.

Name ______________________________

My Pet

Draw a pet.

Draw its food and water.

Food

Water

Notes for Home Your child drew a picture of an animal that would be a good pet and the food and water it needs to live.

Home Activity: Talk with your child about a different kind of pet and the things it needs to stay alive.

Name ____________________

Explore Activity
Unit A Chapter 2

Explore how feathers protect birds.

Draw.

© Scott Foresman K

Notes for Home Your child drew water droplets to show what happens when water is dropped on a feather.
Home Activity: Discuss with your child how feathers protect birds when it rains.

Name ______________________________

Animals and Their Babies

adult

A cow is an adult.

baby

A calf is a baby.

Draw.

adult	baby

Notes for Home Your child drew or cut and pasted a picture of a favorite animal and its baby.
Home Activity: Ask your child to tell how the adult and baby are alike and how they are different.

Name ______________________________

Explore Activity
Unit A Chapter 2

Caring for Baby Animals

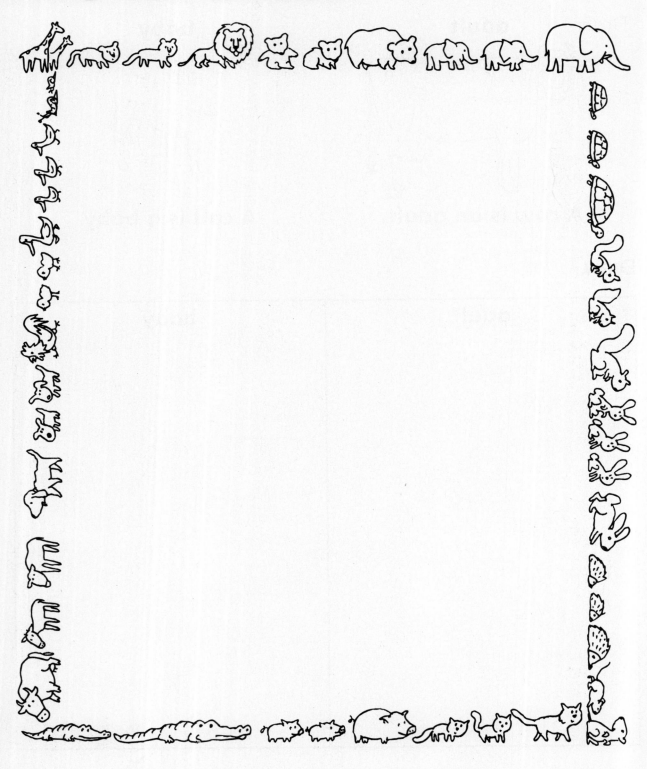

Notes for Home Your child drew a picture of one way a favorite animal takes care of its baby.
Home Activity: Ask your child to share more ways the animal could care for its baby.

Name ______________________________

Explore Activity
Unit A Chapter 2

Explore nests.

Draw.

Notes for Home Your child drew a picture to show a bird nest and how the bird uses the nest to care for its young.
Home Activity: Look for bird nests outside with your child. Talk about what makes a good place for a bird nest.

Name ________________________

Family Activity
Unit A Chapter 3

Dear Family,

Our class will be learning about plants. We will talk about things that plants need to live. We will learn about seeds, roots, stems, leaves, and flowers. In the space, I drew some plants. Look on the other side to find out about some things that you and I can do together to find out more about plants.

Name ____________________

Science at Home

Here are some activities we can do together.

What's the Plant?

I'll think of a plant that I like.
I'll tell you some things about the plant.
You guess the plant.
Then we'll switch.

Windowsill Garden

We'll save seeds from fruits we eat.
You can help me plant them in soil.
We'll give them water and light.
Then we'll watch them grow.

Science in the Community

The next time you and your child do errands, look indoors and outdoors for plants of all shapes and sizes. Encourage your child to show you the leaves and the stems of different plants. Talk with your child about the importance of plants in your community. How are plants used to make the neighborhood look nice? What other important things do plants provide?

Name ______________________

A Sunflower Seed Grows

A sunflower grows.

Look.

Figure out the order.

Use 1, 2, 3, 4 to show the order.

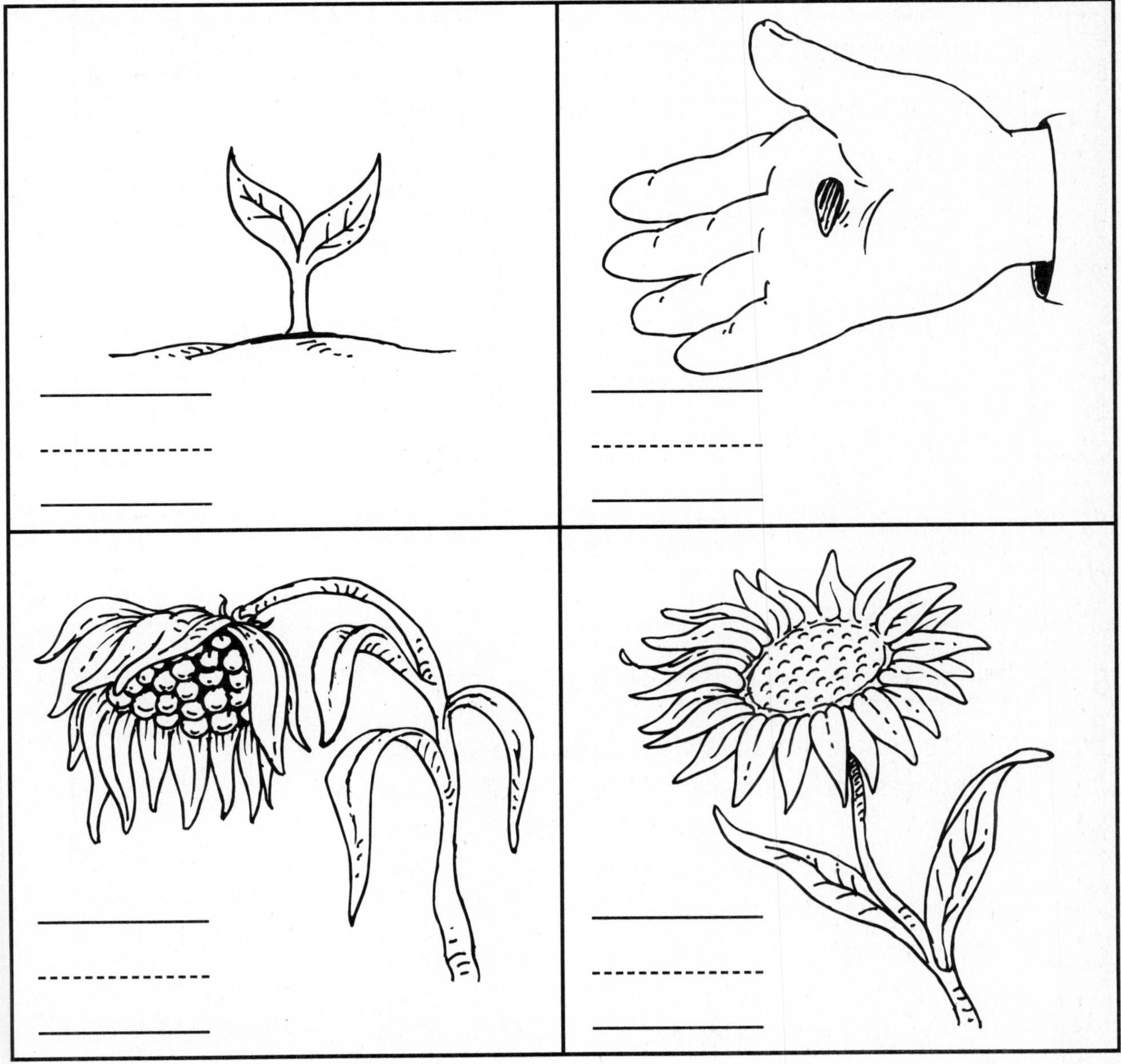

Notes for Home Your child numbered pictures to show how a seed grows into a plant.
Home Activity: Ask your child to point to the picture that shows where seeds for more sunflowers will come from.

Name ______________________

Explore Activity
Unit A Chapter 3

What Will the Seed Become?

Paste a seed.

Draw the plant.

Notes for Home Your child chose a seed and drew a picture showing the plant that will grow from this seed.

Home Activity: Point to an indoor or outdoor plant. Have your child talk about some changes that happen as the plant grows.

Name ______________________________

Explore Activity
Unit A Chapter 3

Explore how seeds move.

Draw.

Circle.

How My Seed Might Move				
	Seed 1		Seed 2	
Float in air	Yes	No	Yes	No
Float on water	Yes	No	Yes	No
Stick to things	Yes	No	Yes	No

Notes for Home Your child tested seeds to show how they move, then circled to show his or her observations. ***Home Activity:*** After walking outside with your child, look for seeds on your clothing or shoes. Talk about why you did or did not find any seeds.

Name ______________________________

Experiment with seeds.

Draw.

Experiment With Seeds		
Observe	**Dry**	**Wet**
1		
2		
3		
4		

Notes for Home Your child drew pictures to show what happened to seeds under different conditions.
Home Activity: Look at a growing plant with your child. Talk about what the plant needs to grow.

Name ______________________________

Explore Activity
Unit A Chapter 3

What a Plant Needs

Draw a plant.
Show something it needs.

Notes for Home Your child drew a plant that is getting something it needs—air, water, or light.
Home Activity: Talk with your child about things that plants need to stay alive.

Name ______________________________

Explore Activity
Unit A Chapter 3

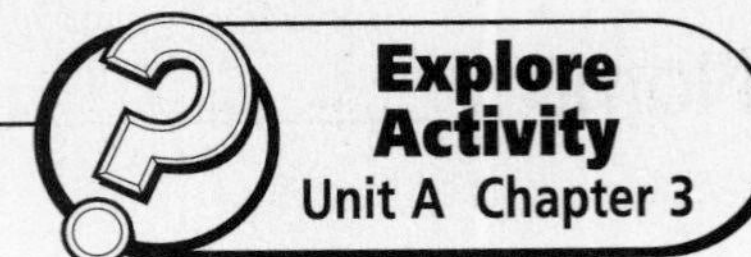

Helping Plants

Help the plant.

Show how.

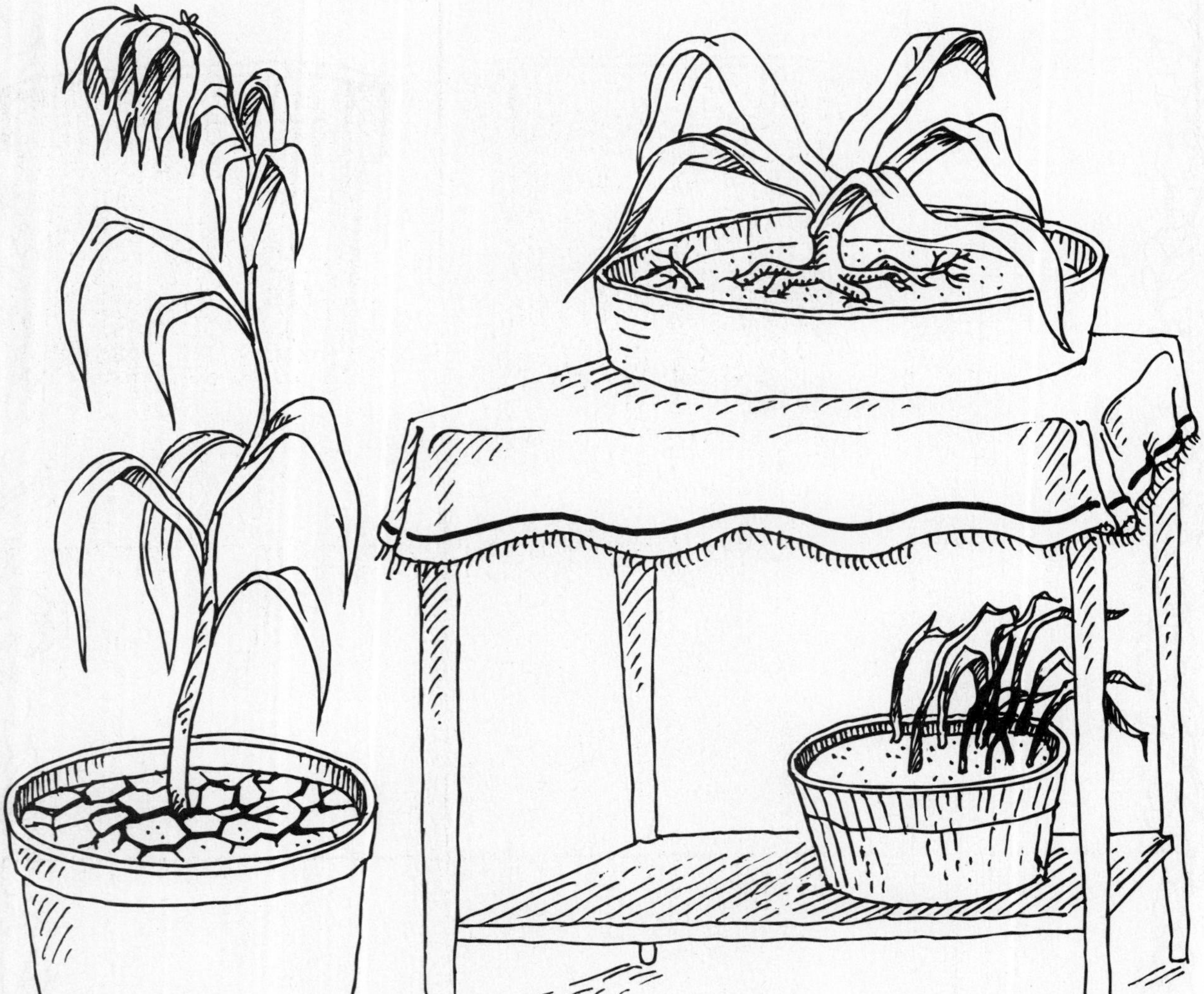

Notes for Home Your child drew pictures showing how he or she could help these plants.
Home Activity: You and your child can look for plants around your home and talk about how to care for them.

Name ______________________

Explore Activity
Unit A Chapter 3

Explore moisture.

 **The Best Pot for Planting** 

Predict		
Observe		

Notes for Home Your child predicted by marking an X under which flower pot will be the best for planting. Then your child marked an X under which pot will be best for planting based on his or her observations.
Home Activity: Have your child use the pictures to explain which pot is best for planting.

Name ______________________________

What plant parts are missing?

Look at each plant.
What part is missing?
Draw it.

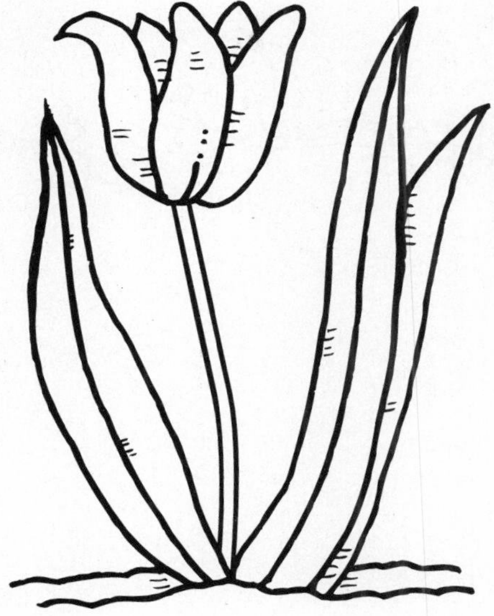

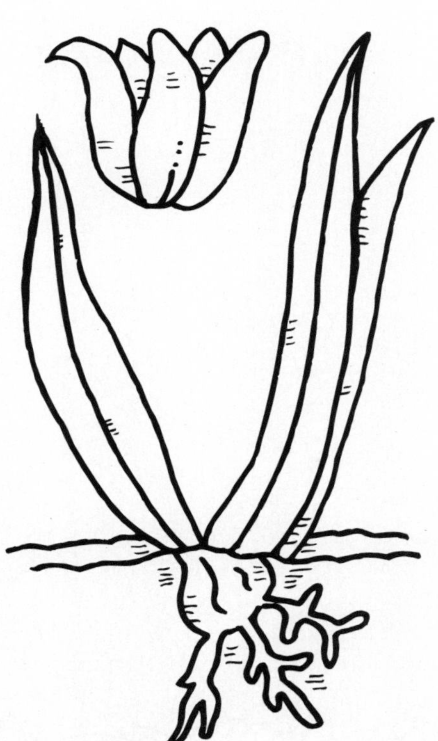

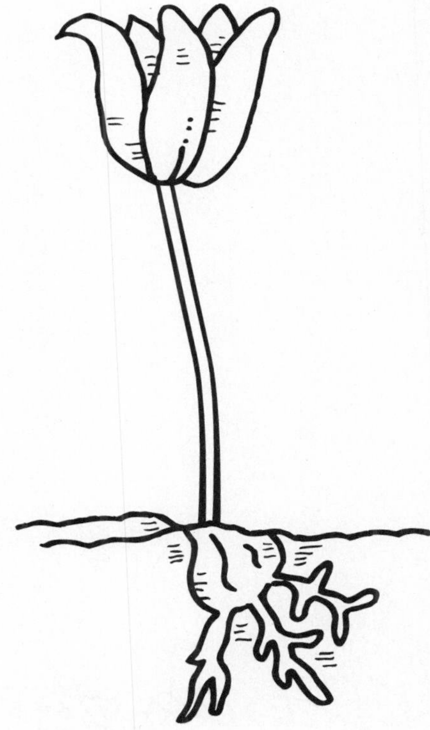

Notes for Home Your child drew the missing part of each plant.
Home Activity: The next time you fix a salad, invite your child to show you some plant parts.

Name ____________________

Explore Activity
Unit A Chapter 3

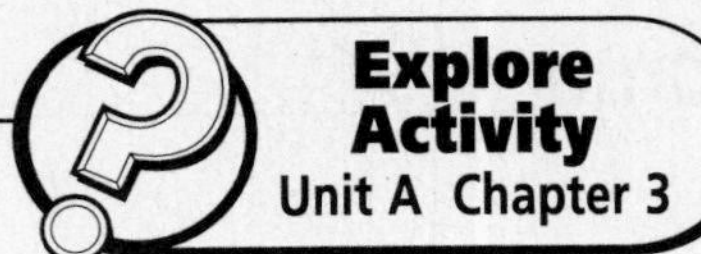

Looking at a Leaf

Make a leaf rubbing.

Tell about the leaf.

Notes for Home Your child made this leaf rubbing.
Home Activity: Look at some leaves with your child. Ask your child to tell you how a plant's leaves help it get what it needs.

Name ______________________

Explore parts of plants.

Draw.

Parts of Plants

Roots	Stems	Leaves	Flowers

Notes for Home Your child observed plants, then drew pictures to record his or her observations.
Home Activity: With your child look at and discuss these parts of a plant: roots, stems, leaves, and flowers.

Name ________________________

Family Activity
Unit B Chapter 1

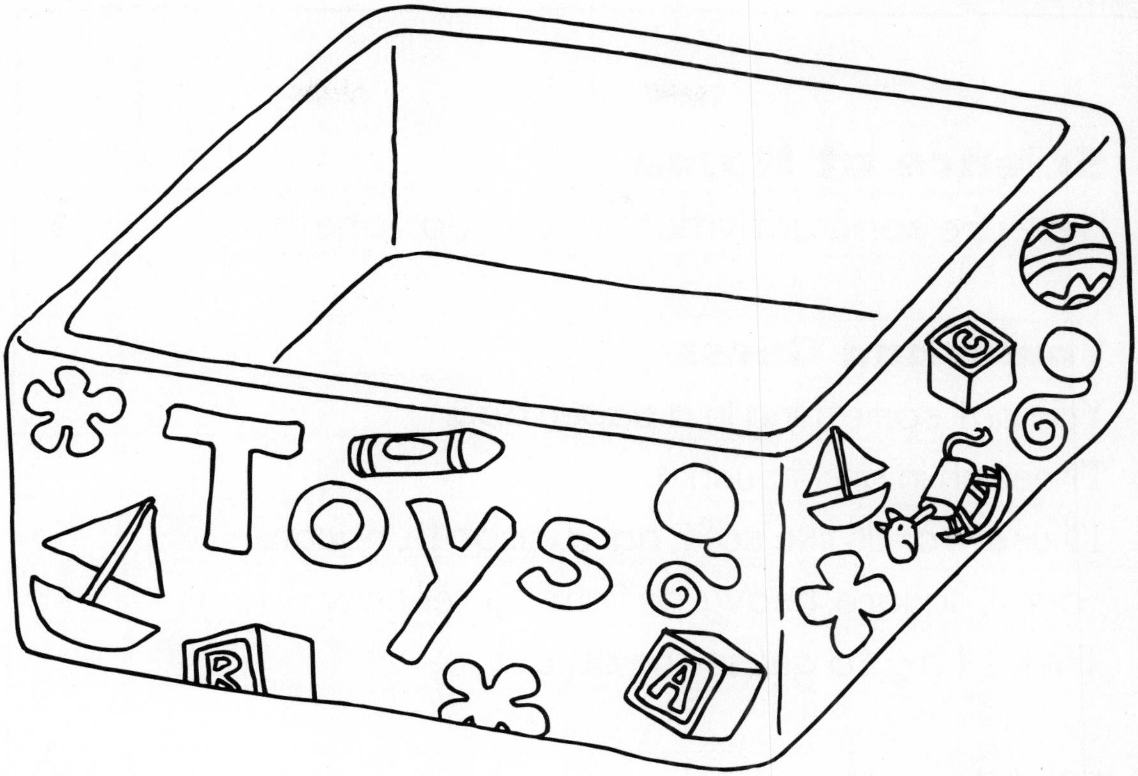

Dear Family,

Our class will be learning about physical science. We will describe how objects look and feel. We will also be comparing the weight of objects and learning that many objects are made up of different parts. In the space, I drew a picture of a toy to help me talk about how the toy looks, feels, and moves. On the back of this page are ideas for activities that you and I can do together to get started learning about the physical characteristics of objects.

Name ____________________

Family Activity
Unit B Chapter 1

Science at Home

Here are some activities we can do together.

Touch and Guess

You put something in a paper bag.
I'll reach in and touch it.
I'll use words like soft, hard, smooth, rough, round, square, heavy, or light to tell how it feels.
Then I'll try to guess the object.

Light or Heavy

First we'll write light or heavy on two cards.
Next, you choose two objects.
I'll hold them to decide which weighs more.
Then I'll put a label by each thing.
Last, I'll choose objects, and you take a turn.

Science in the Community

Gas stations, hardware stores, and supermarkets are great places to explore objects. As you do errands with your child, help him or her become aware of different ways to organize and sort objects using their size, shape, color, or weight. Inviting your child to help you sort laundry or put away groceries will reinforce what he or she is learning about objects, too.

Name ____________________

All About an Object

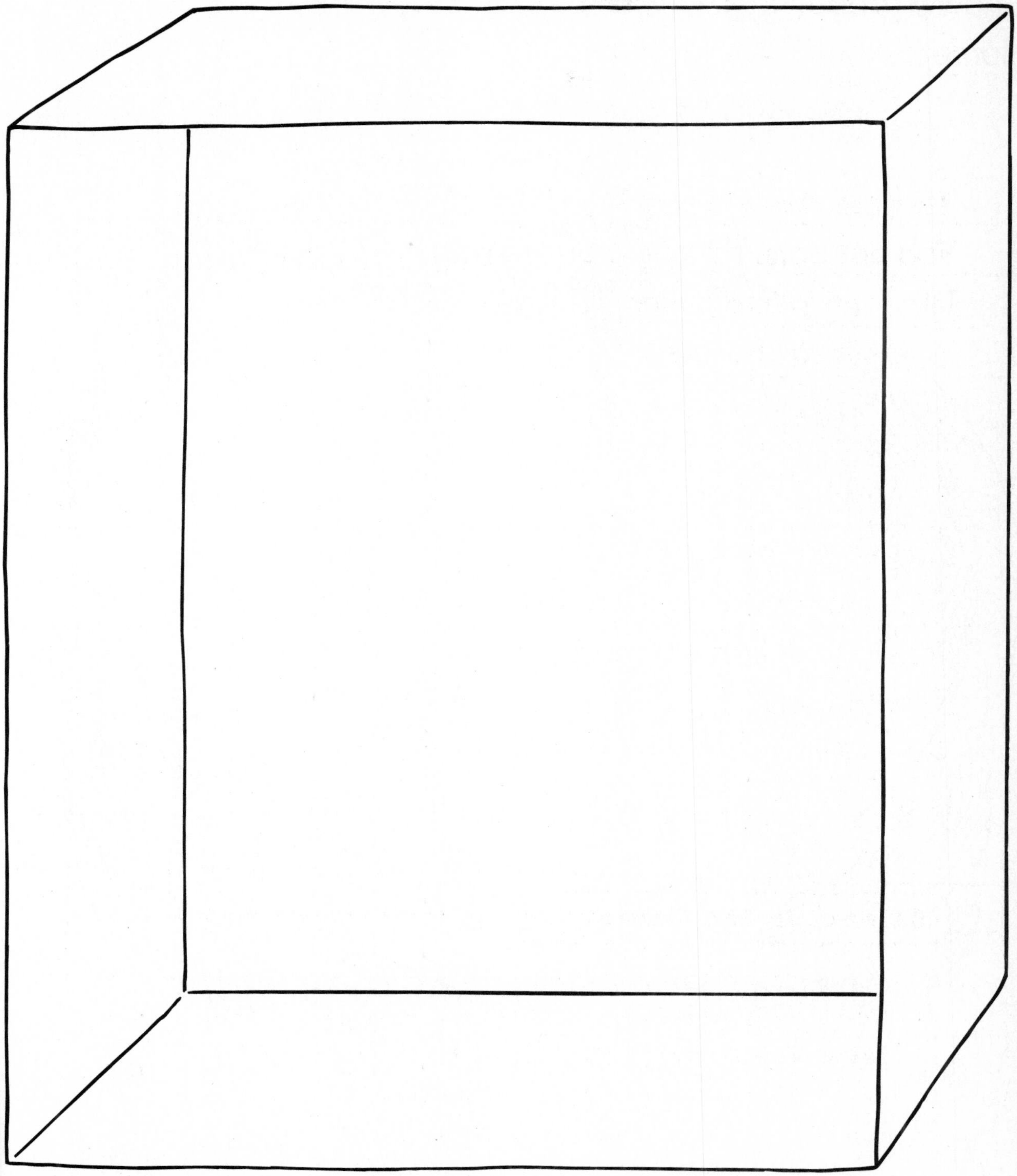

Notes for Home Your child drew an object and described its physical characteristics.
Home Activity: Ask your child to point to an object in your home and describe its size, color, and shape and tell about the way it feels.

Name ________________________________

Explore Activity
Unit B Chapter 1

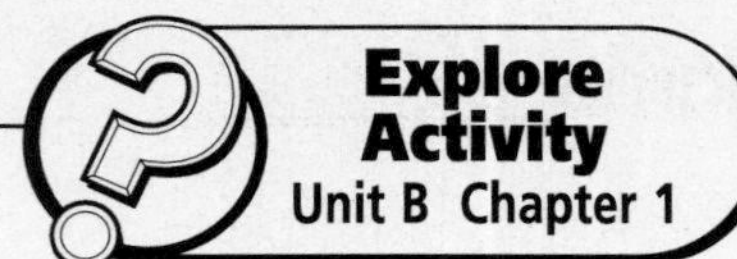

Sorting It All Out

Show a group.

Name it.

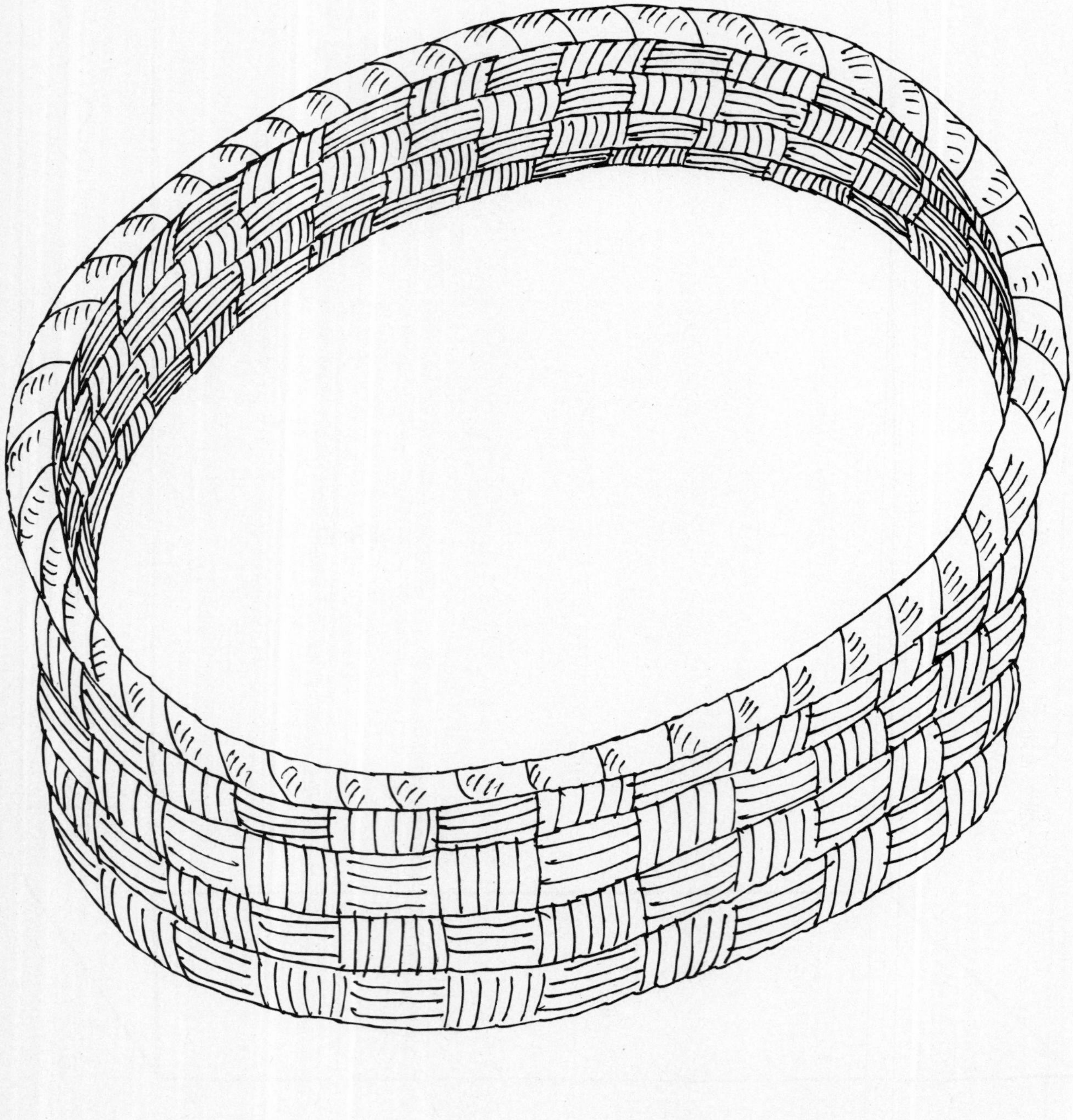

Notes for Home Your child sorted objects and drew a group.
Home Activity: After a meal, involve your child in putting clean dishes or tableware in their proper place. Talk about how your child knew where each thing belonged.

Name ______________________

Explore material.

Draw.

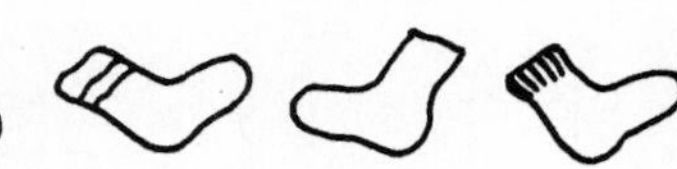

Notes for Home Your child drew a sock to show its characteristics such as color and size.
Home Activity: Invite your child to help sort socks the next time you do laundry. Talk about how your child knows which socks make a pair.

Name ____________________

Explore Activity
Unit B Chapter 1

Light or Heavy?

Draw something light.
Draw something heavy.

Notes for Home Your child identified light and heavy objects.
Home Activity: When putting away toys, have your child pick up two toys and tell which is lighter and which is heavier.

Name ______________________________

Explore Activity
Unit B Chapter 1

Lighter or Heavier?

Draw something lighter than your shoe.
Draw something heavier than your shoe.
Then compare the weights of three more things.

Lighter	My Object	Heavier

Notes for Home Your child compared the weights of three objects.
Home Activity: When preparing a meal, give your child an object and invite him or her to find things in the kitchen that are lighter and heavier than that object.

Name ______________________

Explore weight.

Draw.

Large Object	Small Objects

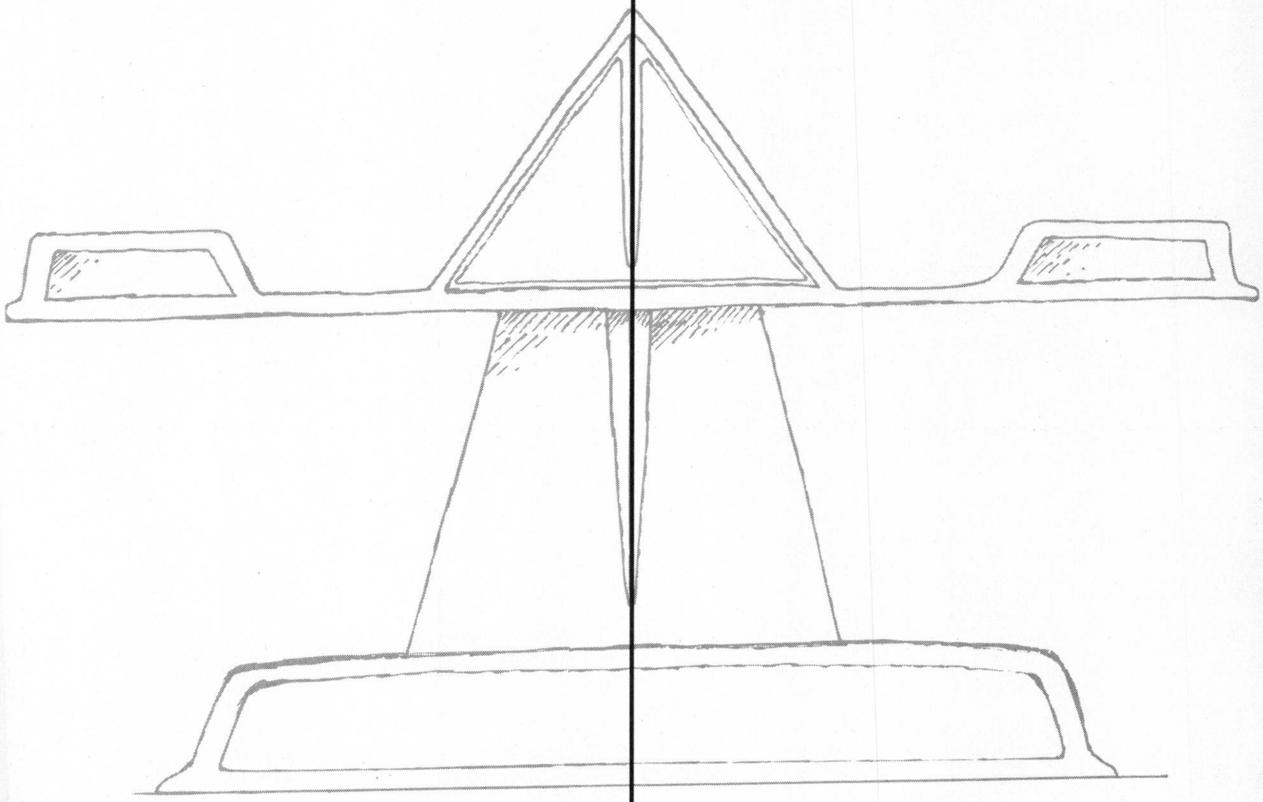

Notes for Home Your child drew pictures to show how many small objects it took to balance a large object. ***Home Activity:*** Talk with your child about how the balance changes when the objects are not balanced. For example, ask: "How does the scale look when only a block is on it?"

Name ____________________

What Part Is Missing?

Draw the missing part.

Notes for Home Your child identified missing parts and drew them.
Home Activity: Invite your child to select a toy. Take turns pointing to and naming the parts of the toy.

Name ______________________________

Making a Snack

Show the parts.

Show how to make the snack.

1.	2.
3.	4.

Notes for Home Your child drew the ingredients needed to make a snack and then showed how to combine them.
Home Activity: Involve your child in helping to make a salad. Have him or her identify each ingredient or part. Then talk about how the parts were put together to make the whole salad.

Name ______________________________

Explore parts of toys.

Draw.

Notes for Home Your child explored toys, then drew one toy and used arrows to show the toy parts that move.
Home Activity: Explore toys at home with your child. Talk about which parts of the toys move and how they move.

Name ______________________________

Family Activity
Unit B Chapter 2

Dear Family,
Our class will be learning about three forms of energy: sound, heat, and light. We will listen for loud and soft sounds. We will compare hot and cold objects. We will learn about things that make light. In the space, I drew a picture of a fire in a fireplace, then I talked about heat and light from a fire. On the back of this page are ideas for activities that you and I can do together to get started learning about sound, heat, and light.

Name ____________________

Family Activity
Unit B Chapter 2

Science at Home

Here are some activities we can do together.

What's That Sound?

Close your eyes.
Listen to the sound I make.
Guess what I used to make the sound.
Then let's switch roles.

Fun with Sun Tea

First we'll fill a quart jar with cold water.
Then we'll put in 2 caffeine-free tea bags.
Next we'll put the jar in the sun for 4 hours.
We'll try it warm and then cold.
Which way do you like your sun tea?

Science in the Community

Help your child become aware of safety sounds and lights in your community. Fire engine and police sirens warn motorists and pedestrians to move out of the way. Traffic lights at intersections tell us when to stop and go. As you are out and about in your neighborhood, talk with your child about these safety sounds and lights. Encourage your child to tell you what each means, and have him or her show you safe ways to walk in the neighborhood.

Name ________________

Softer or Louder?

Draw.

Softer		Louder

Notes for Home Your child drew objects that make softer sounds and louder sounds than a person speaking.
Home Activity: Ask your child to point to objects that make a softer sound and a louder sound than your doorbell.

Name ____________________

Container Shake

Draw.

Softer	Louder

Notes for Home Your child placed objects in containers, shook them, and compared the sounds. Then your child drew pictures to show which was softer and which was louder.
Home Activity: Help your child make shakers by putting small objects in clean, empty cans and covering them with foil. Shake to compare two sounds. Which is softer? Which is louder?

Name ______________________________

Explore sounds.

Draw.

Notes for Home Your child listened to sound-producing objects with and without cylinders and then drew the cylinder and object that created the loudest sound.
Home Activity: Take turns with your child listening to sound-producing objects with and without a cylinder (such as an empty paper towel roll).

Name ______________________________

Explore Activity
Unit B Chapter 2

Is It Hot or Cold?

Draw.

Hot	Cold

Notes for Home Your child drew hot and cold objects.
Home Activity: When eating, ask your child to name some hot foods and some cold foods that are part of the meal.

Name ______________________________

Explore Activity
Unit B Chapter 2

Changes Caused by Heat and Cold

Draw.

Notes for Home Your child drew pictures showing how heat and cold can affect objects.
Home Activity: Have your child observe foods before and after cooking or freezing. Talk about how heat and cold change the foods.

Name ______________________________

Explore Activity
Unit B Chapter 2

Explore ice.

Draw.

What I Think	What I See

Notes for Home Your child filled a balloon with liquid and drew a picture to predict what the liquid would look like after it was frozen. After freezing the balloon, your child drew another picture to show how the liquid looked. ***Home Activity:*** Help your child freeze water in containers of different shapes. Talk about how the cold affects the liquid.

Name ______________________________

Explore Activity
Unit B Chapter 2

Inside and Outside Lights

Draw the missing lights.

Notes for Home Your child identified missing indoor and outdoor lights and drew them.
Home Activity: Talk about the different kinds of lights found in your home. Which room has the most lights?

Name ______________________________

Explore Activity
Unit B Chapter 2

An Important Light

Color the lights.

Use

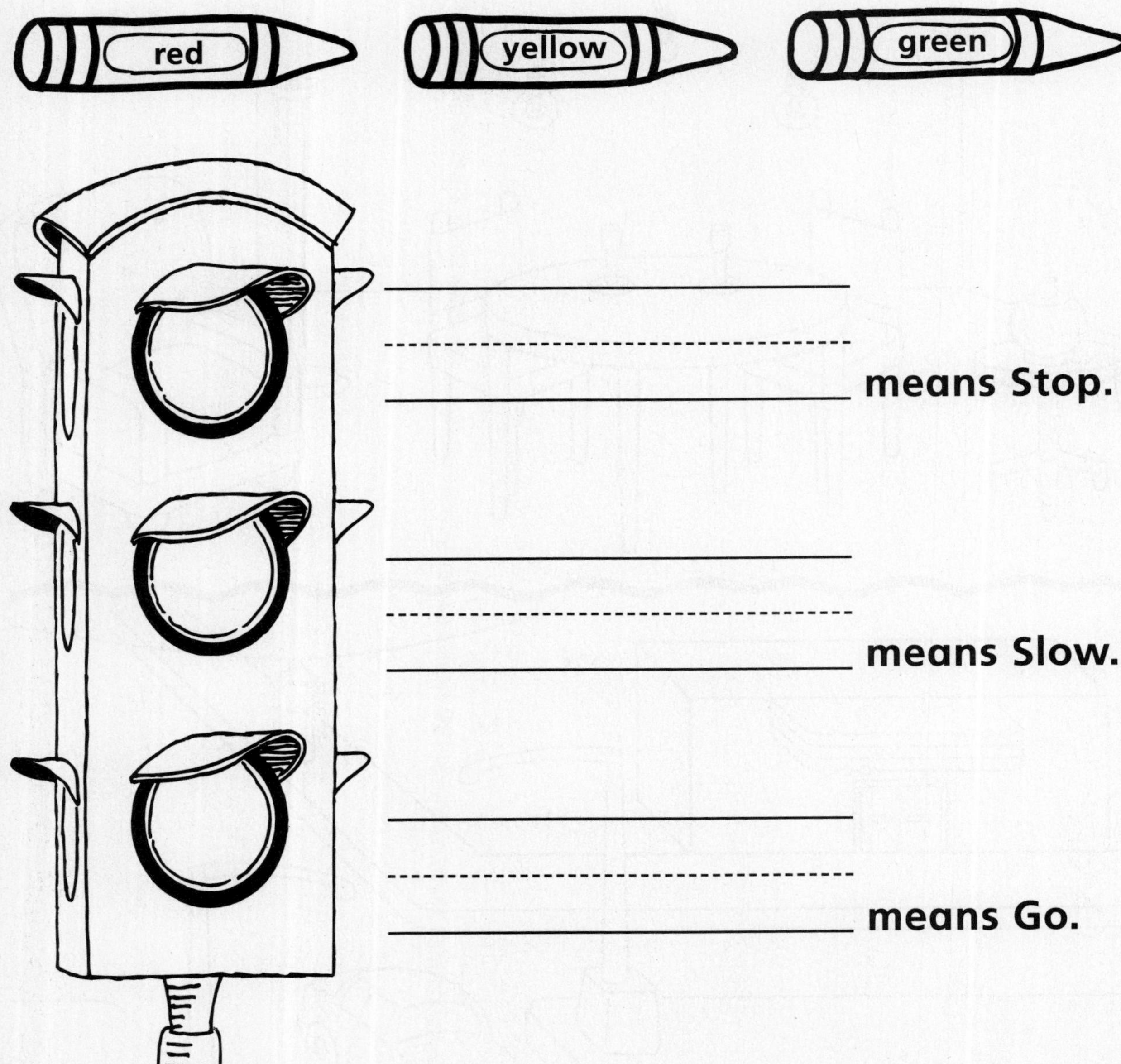

red
yellow
green
means Stop.
means Slow.
means Go.

Notes for Home Your child colored the traffic light.
Home Activity: Point out a traffic light in your neighborhood. Have your child identify the colors and tell what each means.

Name ____________________

Explore Activity
Unit B Chapter 2

Explore light.

Paste.

Notes for Home Your child experimented to find out what happens to a paper with a block on it that is left in the sunlight.
Home Activity: Ask your child to point out the shape on the paper pasted on this page and to tell how the shape was made.

Name ______________________________________

Experiment with a shadow.

Draw.

Notes for Home Your child drew a picture to show the shadow created when a flashlight was shown on a block or other object.

Home Activity: Look for shadows with your child. Talk about where the light source is in relation to the shadow.

Name

Family Activity
Unit B Chapter 3

Dear Family,

Our class will be learning about different kinds of movement. We will talk about ways that objects and people can move. We will learn about objects that float and those that sink. We will also explore the way magnets make some things move. In the space, I drew a picture that shows a way I like to move. On the back of this page are ideas for activities that you and I can do together to find out more about movement.

Name ____________________

Family Activity
Unit B Chapter 3

Science at Home

Here are some activities we can do together.

Copy Cat

Let's stand face-to-face.
I'll make some movements.
You watch and copy them.
Then we'll switch.

Magnet Hunt

How many magnets can we find?
First check the refrigerator door.
Then we can look at cupboards.
If we have letter magnets,
we can make words.

Science in the Community

When riding or walking in the community, point out something that is moving and ask your child to talk about its movement. Encourage your child to look for things that can roll, slide, bounce, or spin. Invite your child to show you ways that he or she can move. What movements are safe to do on a lawn or in a park? What movements are safe on sidewalks or inside stores?

Name ________________________________

Explore Activity
Unit B Chapter 3

Ways to Move

Show how you move.

 She can run.	 He can hop.

I can ______________________.

Notes for Home Your child drew and wrote about ways to move.
Home Activity: Turn on some music and ask your child to march, hop, or tiptoe to the beat. After each type of movement, ask: "How did your arms and legs move?"

Name ____________________

Explore Activity
Unit B Chapter 3

Ways Toys Move

Test the toy.

Show how it moves.

	Bounce	Roll	Spin	Slide
Ball				
Car				
Block				

Notes for Home Your child tested toys to see how they move.
Home Activity: Have your child test a toy to see how it moves. Ask: "Does it bounce, roll, spin, or slide?"

Name ___________________________

Explore Activity
Unit B Chapter 3

Explore movement.

Draw.

Notes for Home Your child drew lines to show how high a ball bounces when dropped from different heights.
Home Activity: Bounce a ball with your child on different surfaces such as grass and cement. Ask: "How does the ball's movement change from one surface to another surface?"

Name ______________________________

Explore Activity
Unit B Chapter 3

Will It Float or Sink?

Draw things that float.
Draw things that sink.

Notes for Home Your child drew objects that float and sink.
Home Activity: Help your child select objects to test in the sink or bathtub.

Name ___________________

Explore Activity
Unit B Chapter 3

Sink the Boat.

Draw your boat.

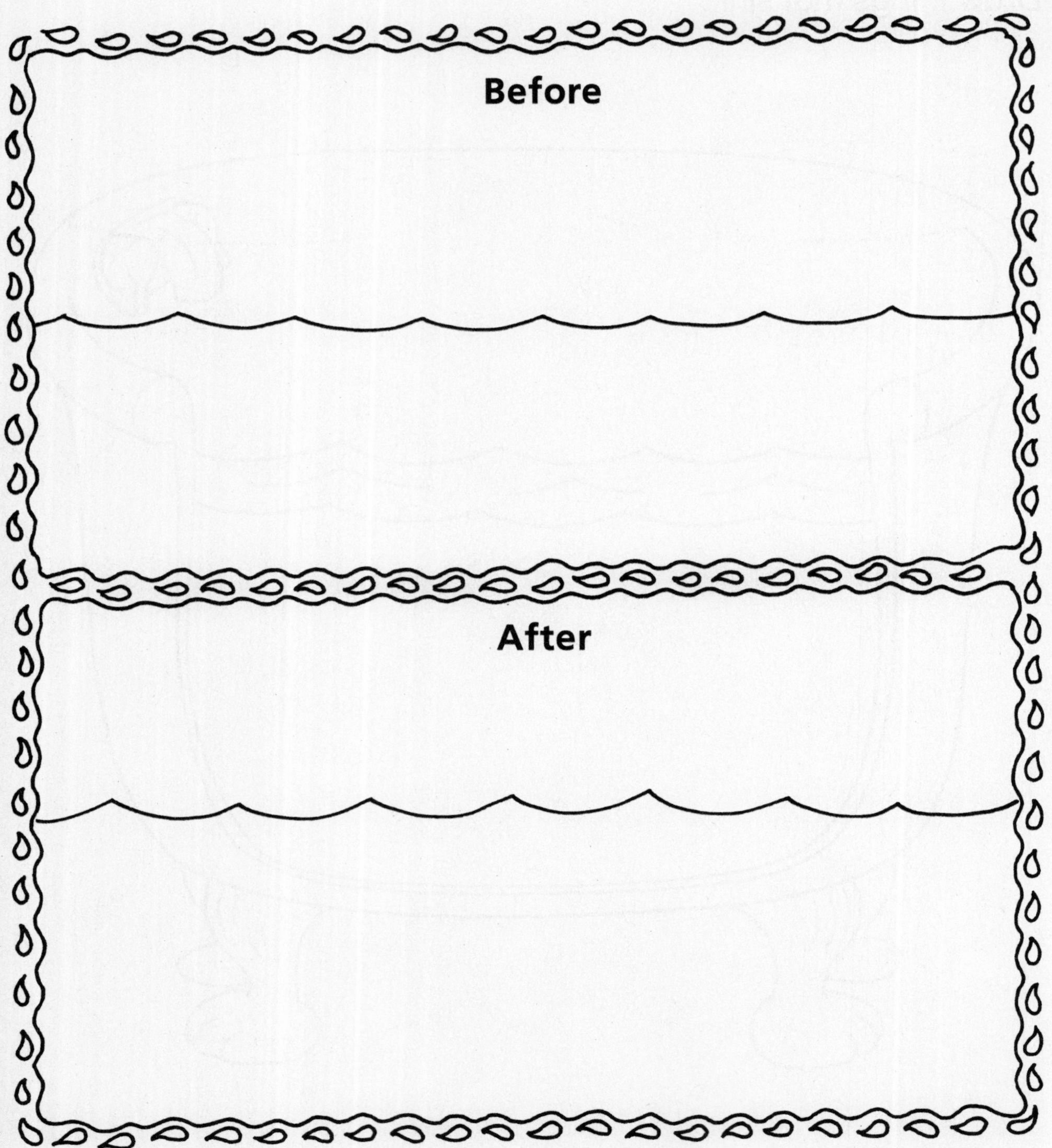

Notes for Home Your child drew a boat before and after sinking it.
Home Activity: Give your child some plastic containers to use in the tub. Talk about how they float and sink.

Name ______________________________

Explore floating and sinking.

Draw.

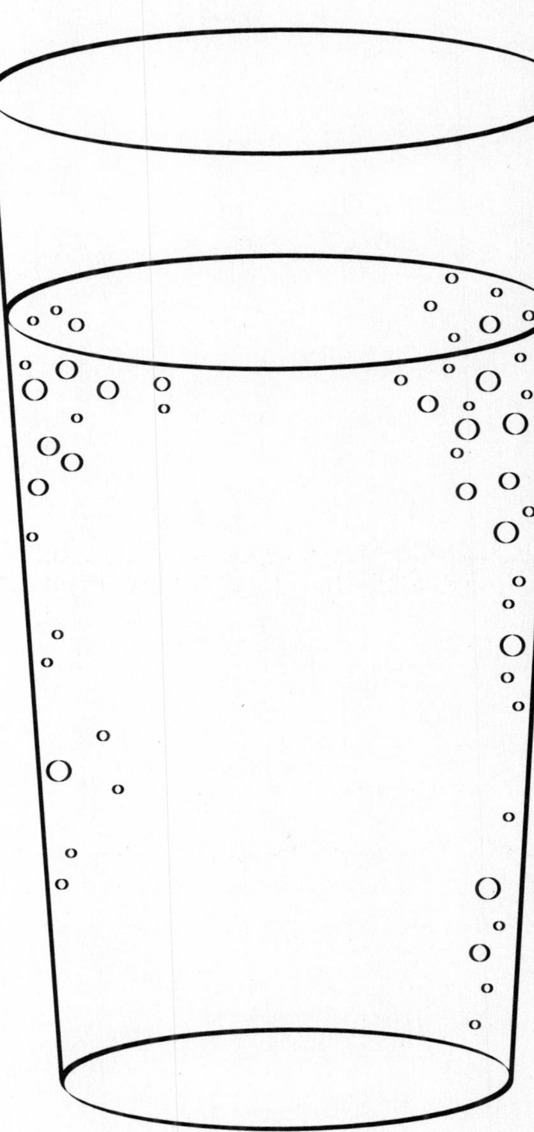

Notes for Home Your child drew pictures to show what happens to raisins in water and in a clear carbonated liquid.
Home Activity: Have your child test other small pieces of fruit in a clear, carbonated liquid to see what happens.

Name ___________________________________

Explore Activity
Unit B Chapter 3

What Will a Magnet Pull?

Draw.

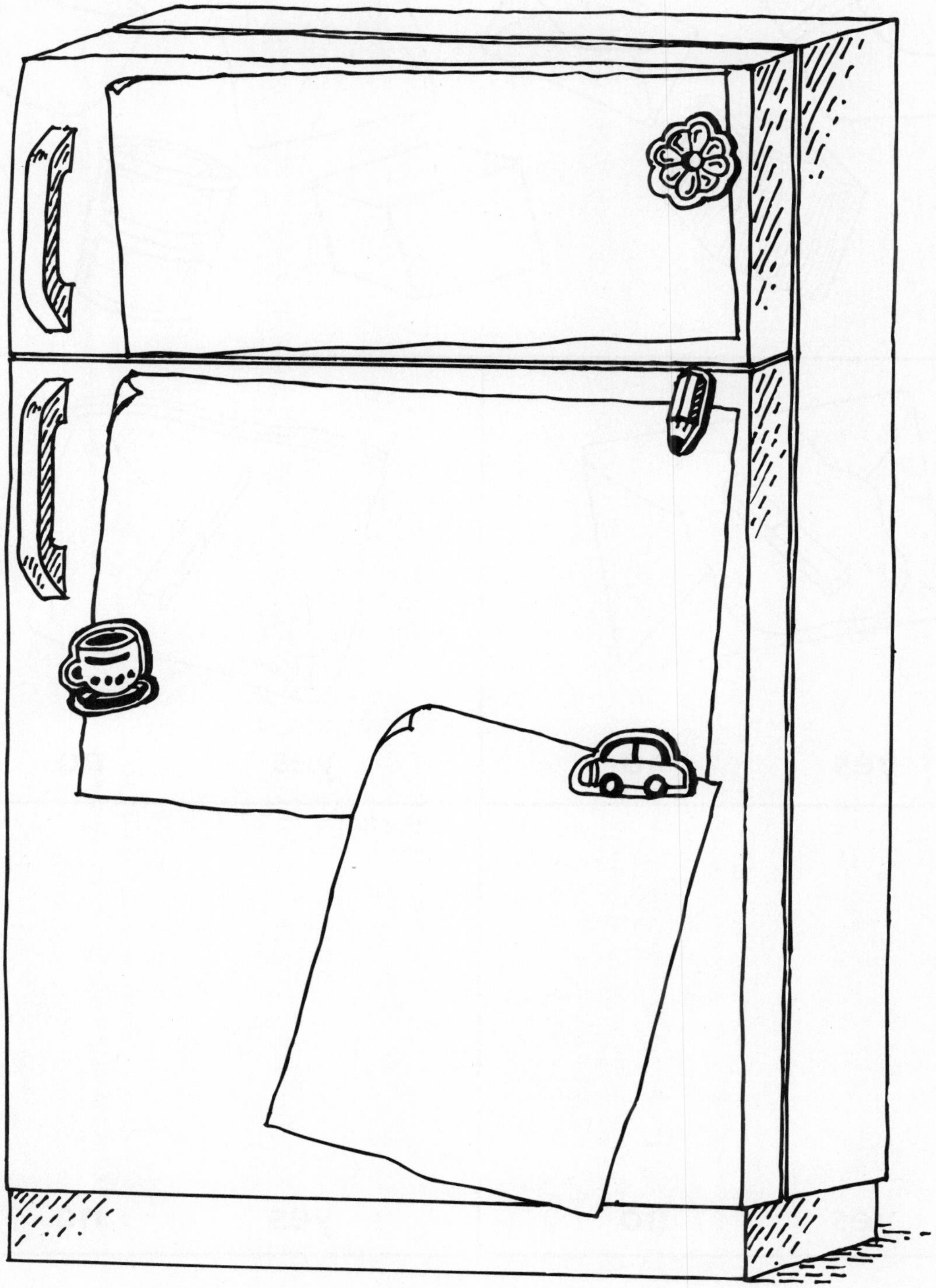

Notes for Home Your child drew objects attracted by magnets.
Home Activity: Help your child find magnets around the house, for example, on cabinet doors and the clasp on a purse.

Name ______________________________

What Can a Magnet Pull Through?

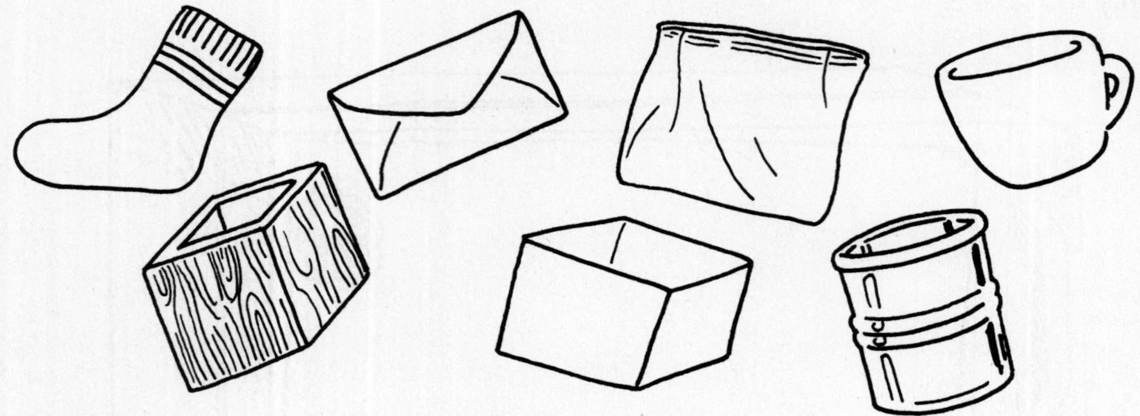

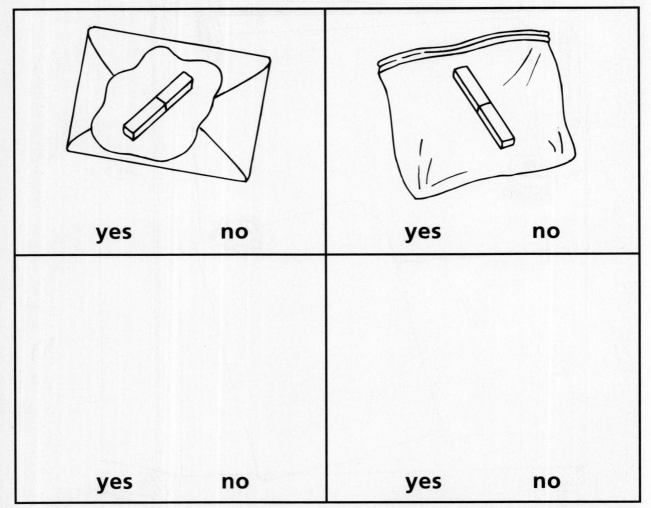

yes no	yes no
yes no	yes no

Notes for Home Your child tested the pull of a magnet through materials such as cloth, paper, plastic, and wood.
Home Activity: Wrap a magnet in foil. Have your child guess and then test if it will attract a paper clip or safety pin through the foil.

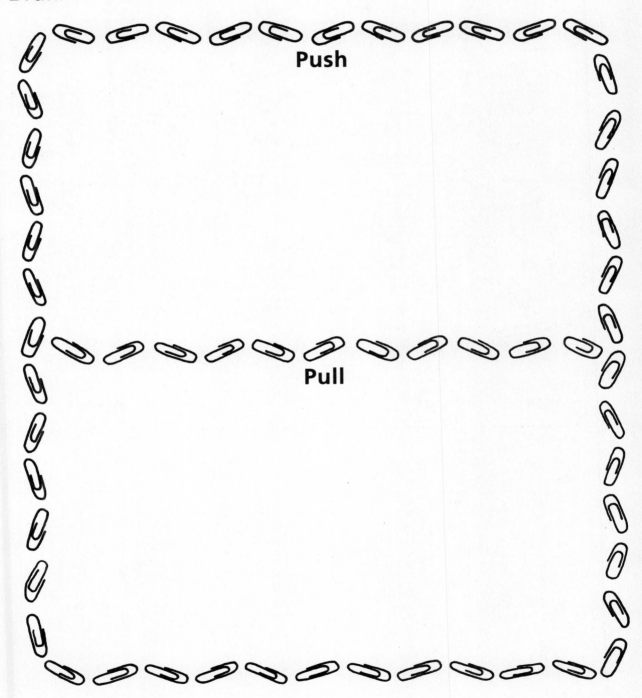

Name ______________________________

Explore pushing and pulling with magnets.

Draw.

Push

Pull

Notes for Home Your child drew pictures to show magnets push and pull each other.
Home Activity: Have your child use a magnet to show how it can pull things such as a paper clip.

Name

Family Activity
Unit C Chapter 1

Dear Family,
Our class will be learning about Earth and the sky. We will talk about landforms and bodies of water. We will also learn about things seen in the daytime sky and the nighttime sky. I drew a picture of a place where I would like to hike. Look on the other side to find out about things that you and I can do together to find out more about Earth and the sky.

Name ______________________

Science at Home

Here are some activities we can do together.

Moon Walk

We can look at the moon
each night for a week.
I'll draw what I see.
We can talk about how the moon seems to change.

Pictures in the Sky

We can look at clouds in the sky.
What shapes or pictures do we see?
How do the clouds move and change?
What other things can we see in the sky?

Science in the Community

When traveling around your community, alert your child to some of the landforms and bodies of water that are present. Depending on where you live, you may be able to point out hills, valleys, mountains, plains, lakes, rivers, or streams. If possible, take photographs of these features. Your child can use them to make a scrapbook of your area. With your help, he or she can label each body of water and landform and share the scrapbook with other family members.

Name ________________________________

Nearby Landforms

Draw.

Notes for Home Your child drew and labeled two landforms in your community.
Home Activity: If possible, visit these landforms with your child. Talk about what you observe.

Name ______________________________

Explore Activity
Unit C Chapter 1

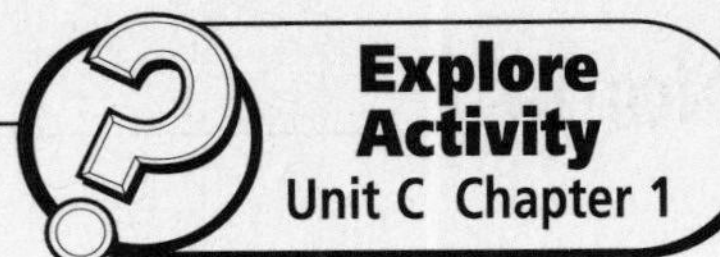

Visiting a Body of Water

Draw.

Notes for Home Your child drew and labeled a body of water.
Home Activity: If possible, take your child to visit a nearby lake, river, or stream.

Name ______________________________

Explore water flow.

Draw.

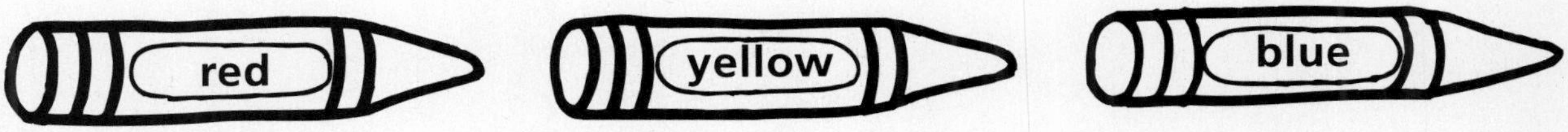

red yellow blue

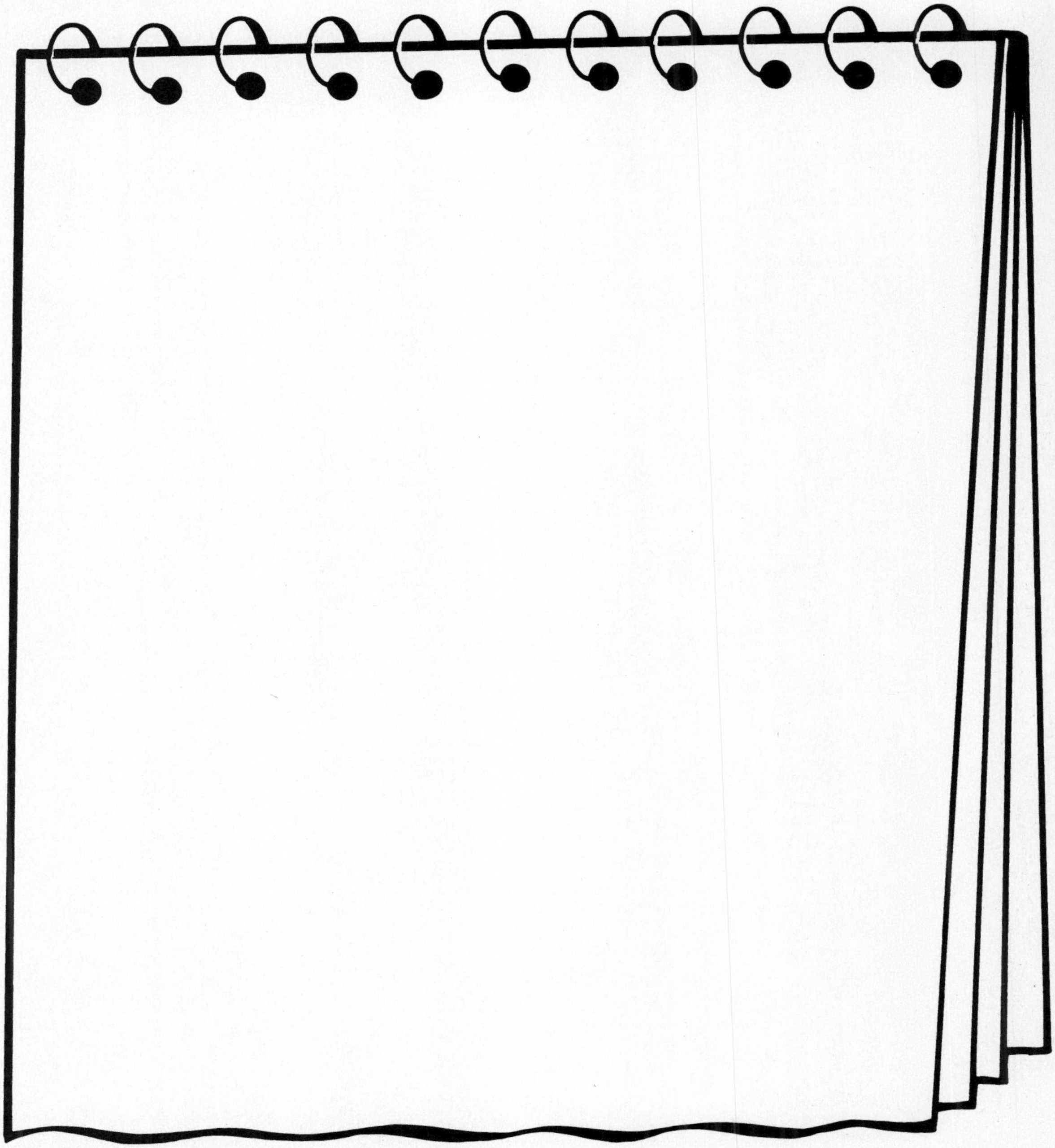

Notes for Home Your child used a different color to show the water flow after water was poured from the top of a landform three different times.
Home Activity: Have your child pour water over various tub toys and talk about how the water flows.

Name ___________________________

Things I Saw in the Daytime Sky

Color.

Draw.

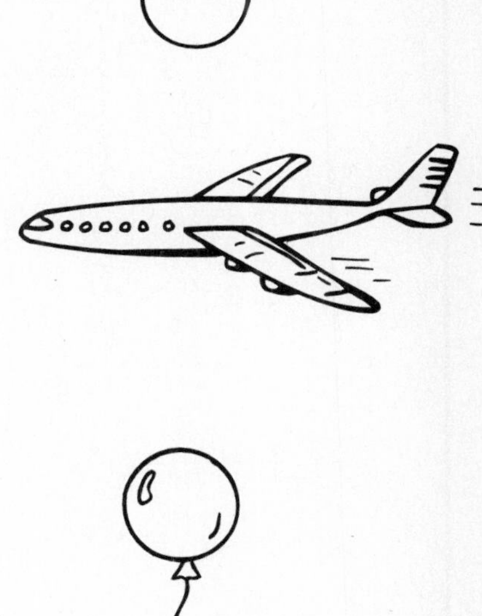

Notes for Home Your child colored and drew objects that he or she saw while looking at the sky. ***Home Activity:*** Look out a window with your child. Take turns naming things that you see in the daytime sky.

Name ____________________

Explore Activity
Unit C Chapter 1

My Daytime Activities

Draw.

Early Morning
Noon

Notes for Home Your child drew pictures to show the position of the sun in the morning and at noon. ***Home Activity:*** If possible, watch a sunrise or a sunset with your child. Talk about where the sun is in the sky. How does the sky change?

Name ______________________________

Explore Activity
Unit C Chapter 1

Explore the sky.

Draw.

Notes for Home Your child used a viewer and then drew pictures of what was observed in the daytime sky.
Home Activity: Ask your child to model how to use a paper towel roll as a viewer. Take turns using the viewer and talking about what you see.

Name ______________________________

Explore Activity
Unit C Chapter 1

The Nighttime Sky

Draw.

Notes for Home Your child drew objects that he or she might see in the nighttime sky.
Home Activity: If possible, view the night sky with your child. Talk about what you observe.

Name ______________________________

Daytime and Nighttime

Draw.

Notes for Home Your child drew and labeled daytime and nighttime pictures.
Home Activity: Have your child look out the same window during the day and again after dark. Talk about how the sky and the view seem to change.

Name ______________________________

Explore Activity
Unit C Chapter 1

Explore star patterns.

Make dots.

Draw.

Notes for Home Your child made and then connected dots to show star patterns.
Home Activity: If possible, on a clear dark night, look for and talk about star patterns with your child.

Name ______________________________

Dear Family,

Our class will be learning about weather and seasons. We will talk about different weather and how weather affects what people wear and do. We will also learn about the four seasons. In the space, I drew a picture of my favorite time of year. The other side has ideas for things that you and I can do together to find out more about the weather and the seasons.

Name ____________________

Science at Home

Here are some activities we can do together.

A TV Weather Forecast

We can watch a weather forecast on the news.
The next day we can observe the weather.
Was the forecast right?
Did the weather differ from the forecast?

Family Fun in Different Seasons

I'll fold a paper in four to make a little book.
We can talk about how our family has fun each season. I'll draw four pictures to show this.
You can help me write spring, summer, fall, and winter.

Science in the Community

When traveling around your community, alert your child to symbols in the community that help people stay informed about weather. For example, point out time and temperature displays on a local bank. Also look for natural and man-made signs of the seasons. For example, in the fall you might help your child notice the leaves changing color or the type of seasonal clothing on display in store windows.

Name ______________________

Explore Activity
Unit C Chapter 2

What's the Weather?

Show the weather.

____

The weather is ______________________.

____

The weather is ______________________.

Notes for Home Your child drew and labeled pictures showing two types of weather.
Home Activity: Talk about today's weather. How does it compare to yesterday's weather?

Name ______________________________

What Will I Wear?

Draw.

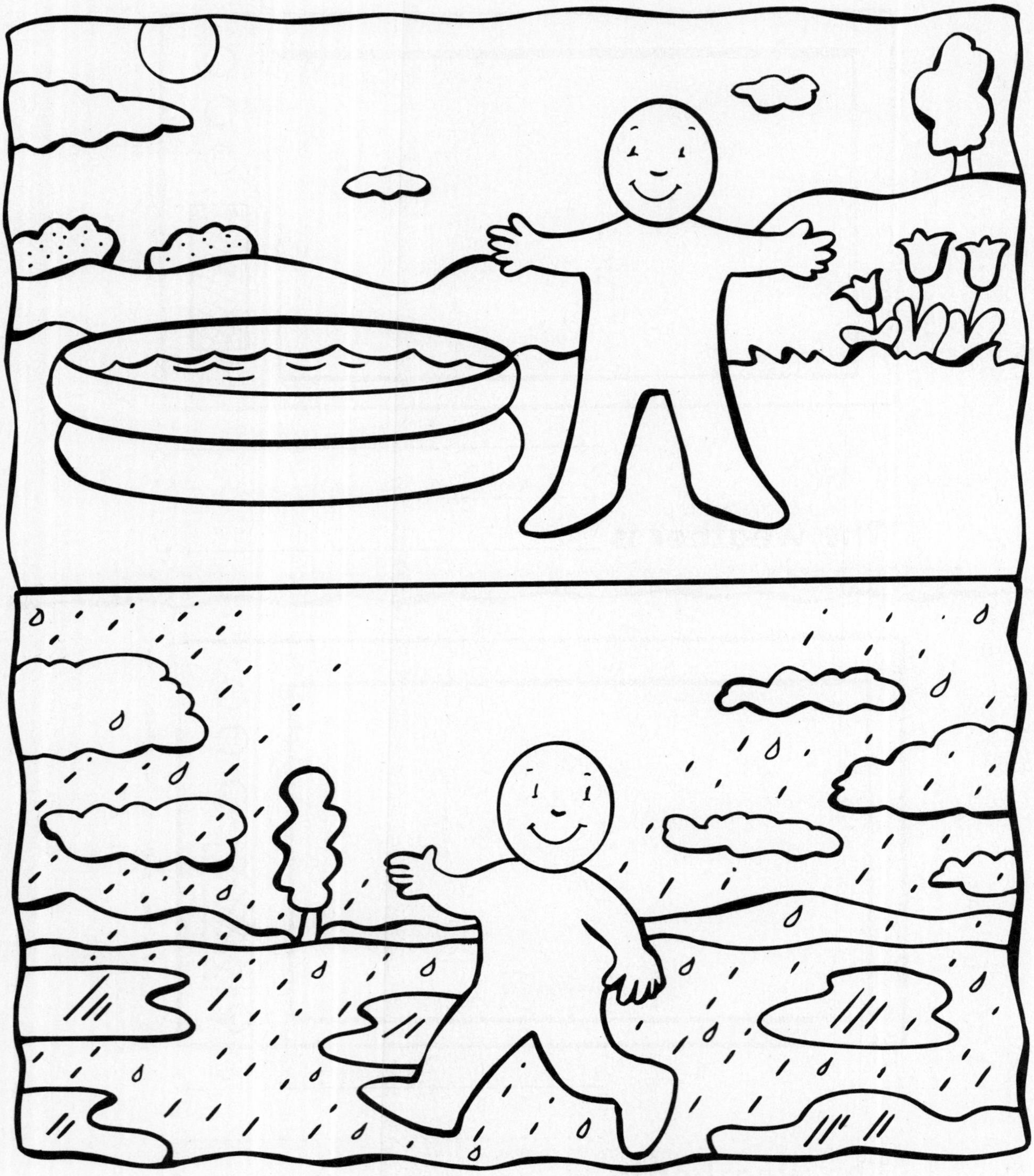

Notes for Home Your child drew what he or she would wear on a hot sunny day and on a rainy day.
Home Activity: Have your child tell about today's weather and what he or she should wear today.

Name ____________________

Explore waterproof material.

Draw.

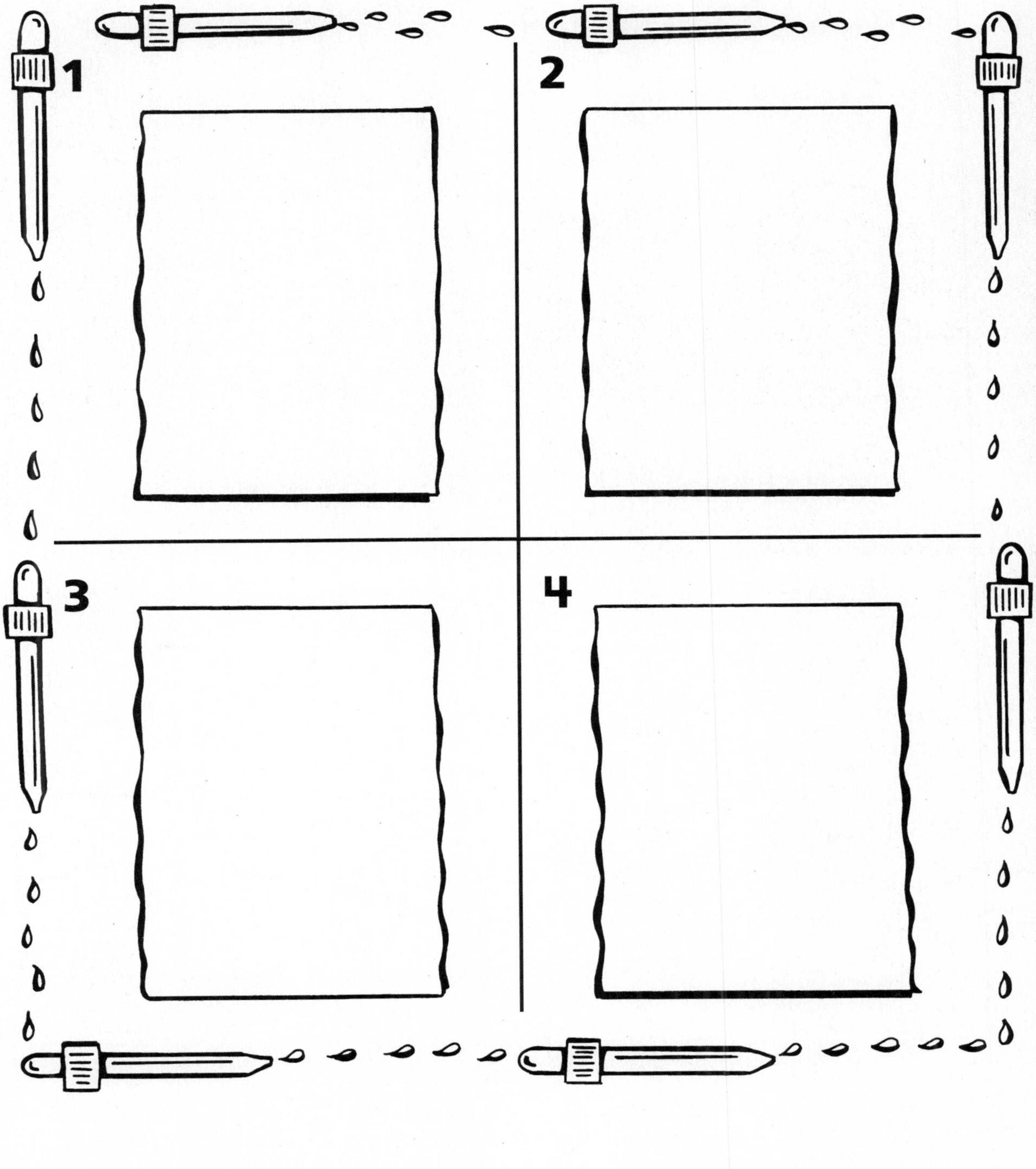

1

2

3

4

Notes for Home Your child tested fabric, then recorded the size of the water spot.
Home Activity: Help your child test a brown paper bag and a plastic bag to see which is more waterproof. Talk about which bag would make a better makeshift rain poncho.

Name ______________________

Explore Activity
Unit C Chapter 2

My Favorite Season

Write.

Draw.

____

Dear ______________________,

____

This shows ______________________ where I live.

Your friend,

____

Notes for Home Your child drew and wrote about his or her favorite season.
Home Activity: Have your child name another season and describe it.

Name ______________________________

Explore Activity
Unit C Chapter 2

My Daily Weather Record

Draw.

Notes for Home Your child drew symbols to show the weather for five days.
Home Activity: Look at the weather report in the local newspaper. Talk with your child about the weather symbols.

Name ____________________

Explore Activity
Unit C Chapter 2

Explore evaporation.

Draw.

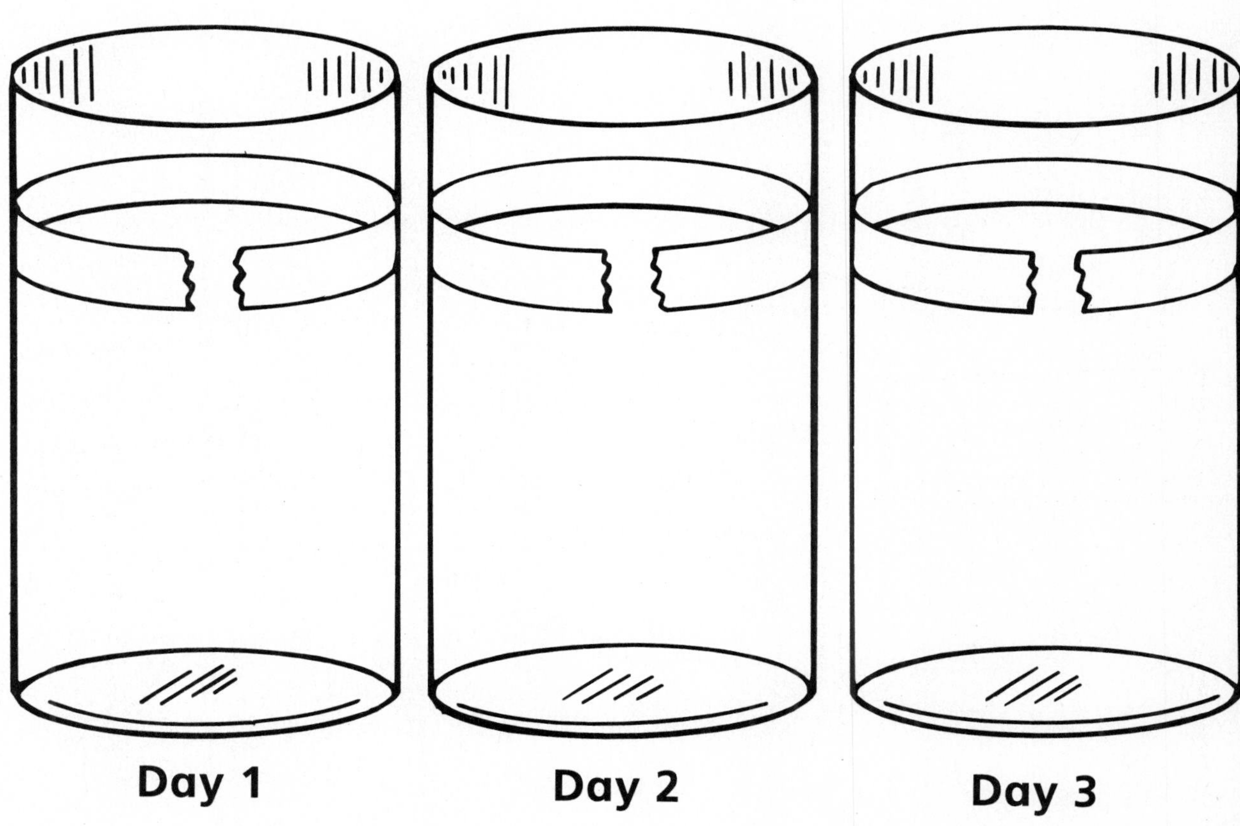

Notes for Home Your child talked about evaporation and drew water to show how the water level in a glass changed each day.
Home Activity: The next time it rains, look for puddles with your child. Notice the size of the puddle, then go back later and talk about how the puddle has changed.

Name

Family Activity
Unit C Chapter 3

Dear Family,
Our class will be learning about caring for the earth. We will find out about natural resources, such as air, water, soil, forests, and oil. We will also talk about how people can conserve and recycle these natural resources. In the space, I drew a picture showing one of the earth's resources. The other side of this letter has ideas for things that you and I can do together to find out more about how people can care for the earth.

Name

Science at Home

Here are some activities we can do together.

Saving Electricity

I can make signs reminding us to turn off lights.
We can also work together to dust lightbulbs.
Clean bulbs use less energy than dirty ones!

Recycling Shopping Bags

I'll decorate some supermarket bags.
We can reuse the bags when we buy groceries.
We can reuse the bags when we do other errands.
I'll remember to say, "No thanks!" to bags I don't need.

Science in the Community

Talk with your child about recycling in your community. Help him or her identify items that can be recycled from your household. You might work together to set up bins for sorting these items.

Name ______________________________

Explore Activity
Unit C Chapter 3

Put Your Stamp on It

Draw.

Notes for Home Your child designed a postage stamp showing a natural resource.
Home Activity: Ask your child to tell why this natural resource is important.

Name ______________________________

Ways We Use Wood

Draw.

Notes for Home Your child drew objects made of wood, which is an important natural resource.
Home Activity: Have your child look around your home and identify some objects made from wood.

Name ______________________________

Explore oil and water.

Draw.

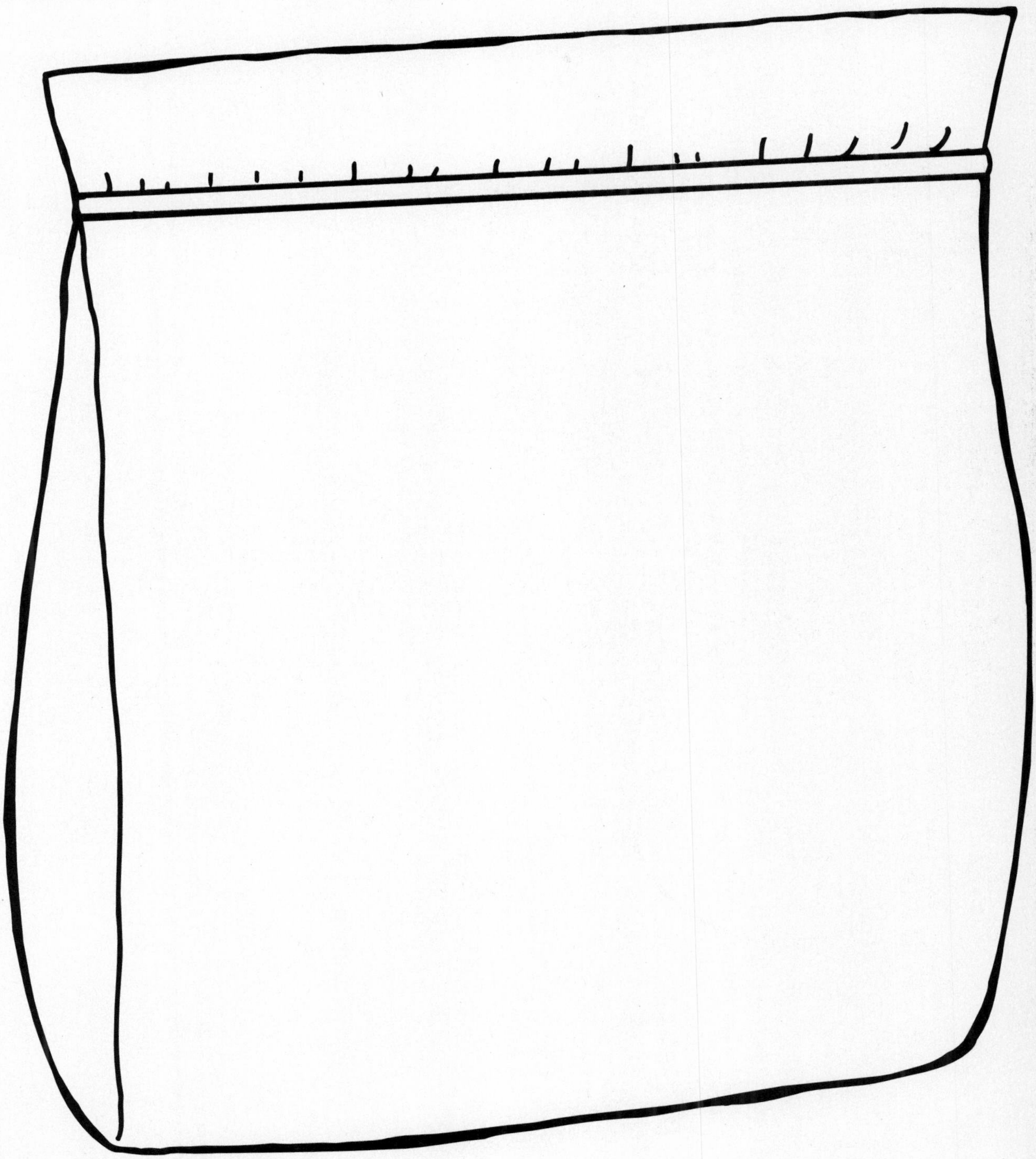

Notes for Home Your child drew a picture to show what happens when you try to mix oil and water. ***Home Activity:*** The next time you are at a gas station with your child, ask a mechanic to explain how to dispose of used oil so it does not get dumped into local water.

Name ______________________

Explore Activity
Unit C Chapter 3

Energy Pledge

Draw.

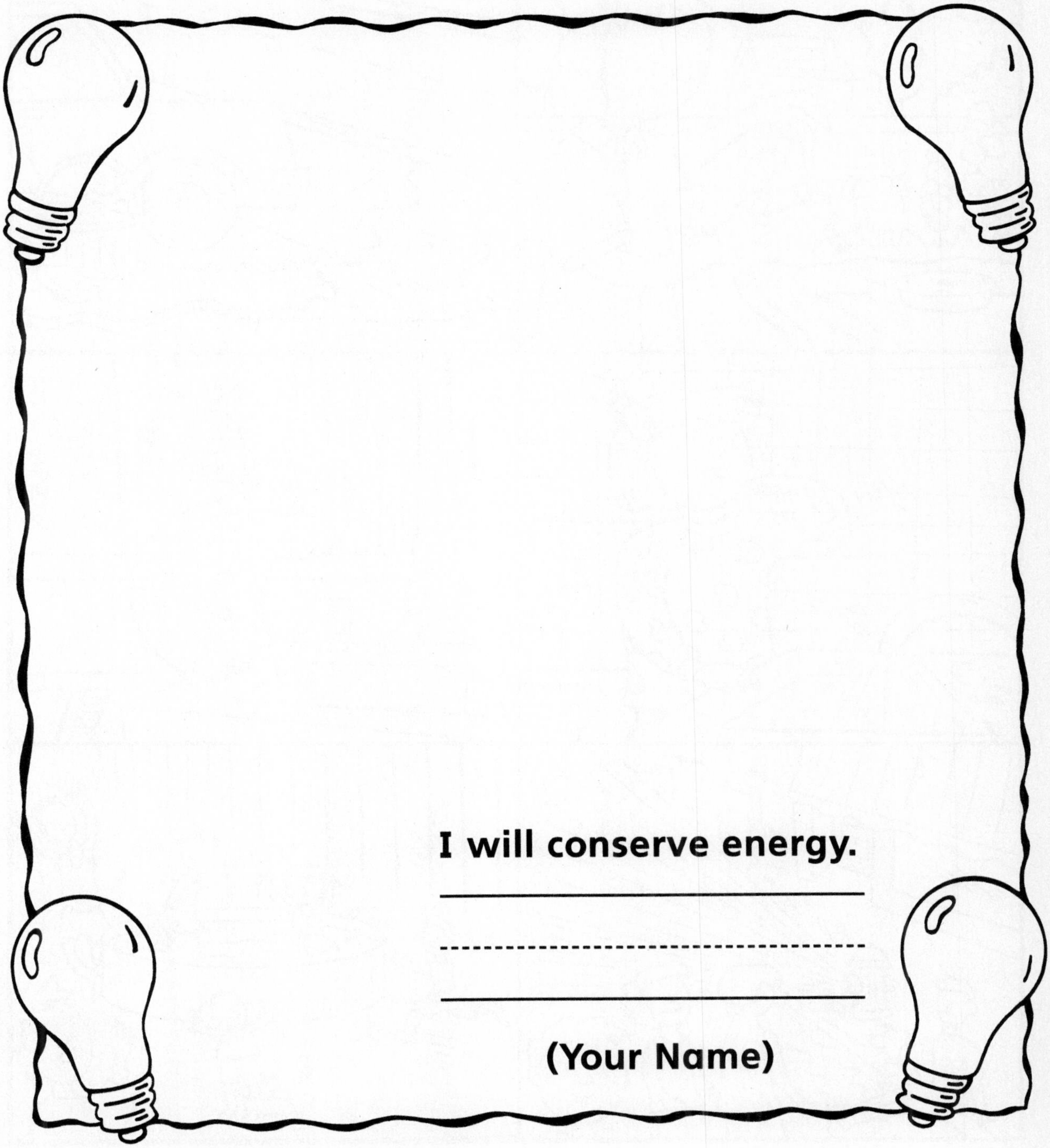

I will conserve energy.

____

(Your Name)

Notes for Home Your child drew something that he or she could do to conserve energy.
Home Activity: Encourage your child to share this energy pledge with other family members.

Name ______________________________

Conserving Water

Notes for Home Your child colored pictures to show water savers and crossed out pictures to show water wasters.

Home Activity: Ask your child to tell you how people can save water while brushing their teeth.

Name ______________________________

Explore Activity
Unit C Chapter 3

Explore water flow.

Draw.

Notes for Home Your child drew pictures to show water flow through a pin hole when the top is on the bottle and when the top is off the bottle.
Home Activity: Help your child learn to turn a water faucet handle to control water flow. Discuss how the water should be flowing from the faucet to help conserve water.

Name ______________________________

Experiment with filtering water.

Draw.

Paper

Pebbles

Notes for Home Your child drew pictures to show how dirty water looked after it was filtered through paper and through pebbles.
Home Activity: Talk with your child about other filters such as a furnace filter. Ask: "Why do you think a furnace has a filter?"

Name ______________________

Let's Recycle!

Draw.

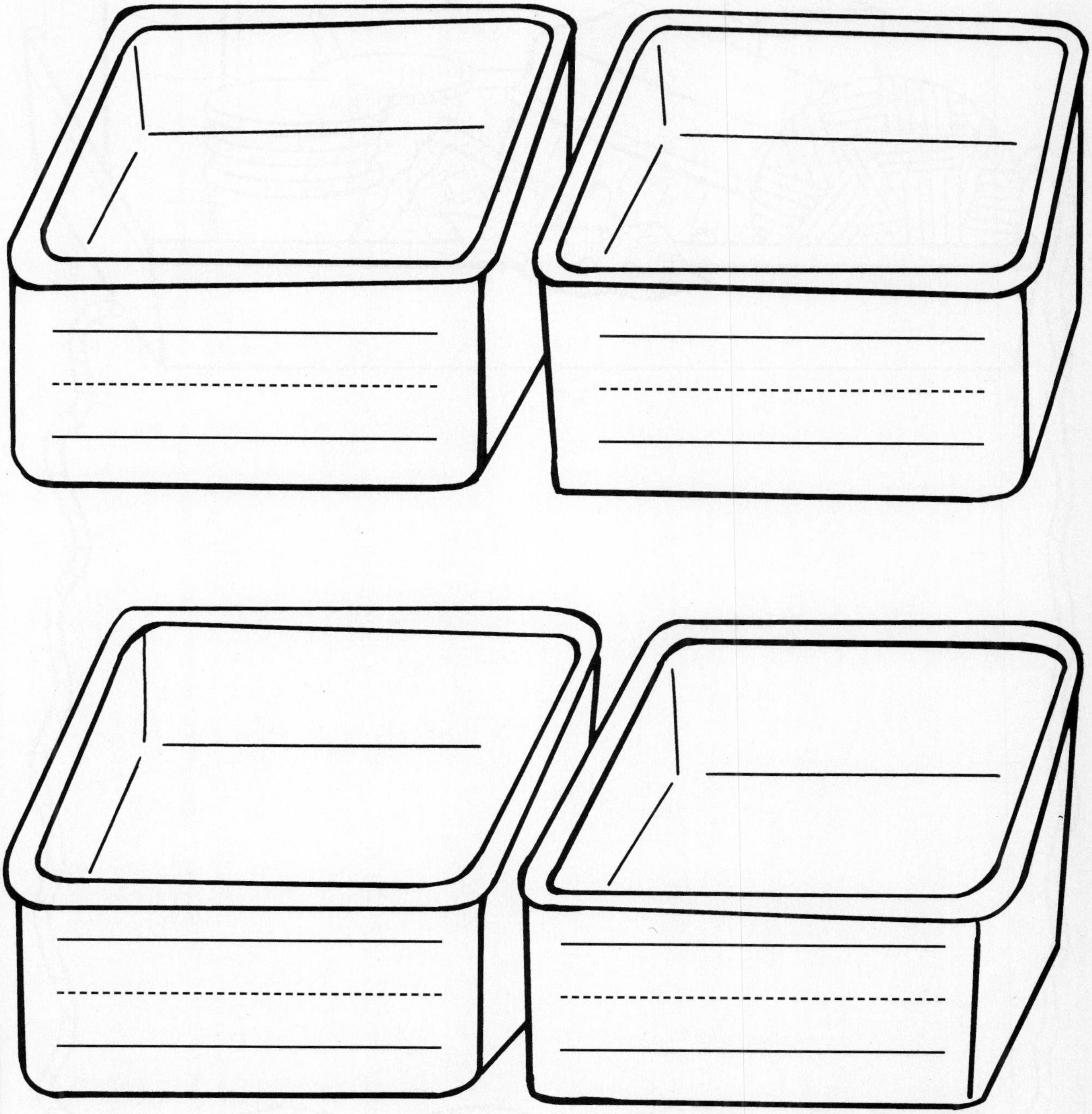

Notes for Home Your child labeled each bin and then drew pictures to show what can be recycled.
Home Activity: Suggest your child decorate a small box for recycling paper, then use the blank side of the paper from the recycling box for phone messages and notes.

Name ______________________________

Treasures from Trash

Draw.

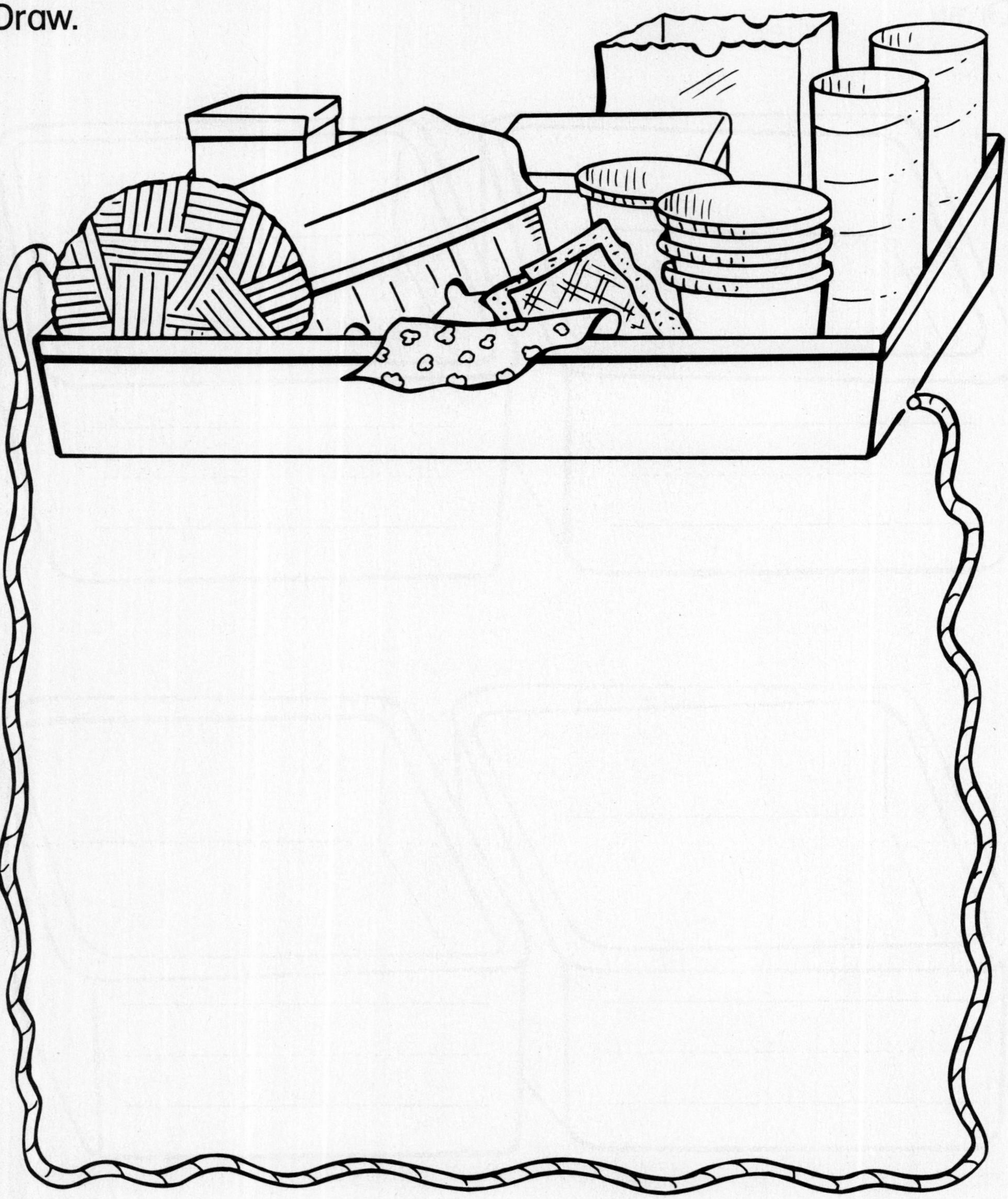

Notes for Home Your child drew something made from recycled items.
Home Activity: Involve your child in recycling small boxes, cans, and plastic cartons at home.

Name ____________________

Explore Activity
Unit C Chapter 3

Explore packaging.

Draw.

No packaging	1 package	2 or more packages

Notes for Home Your child evaluated product packaging and drew pictures to show how some products are packaged.
Home Activity: The next time you go food shopping with your child, ask: "Which of our groceries have the least packaging."

Name________________________________

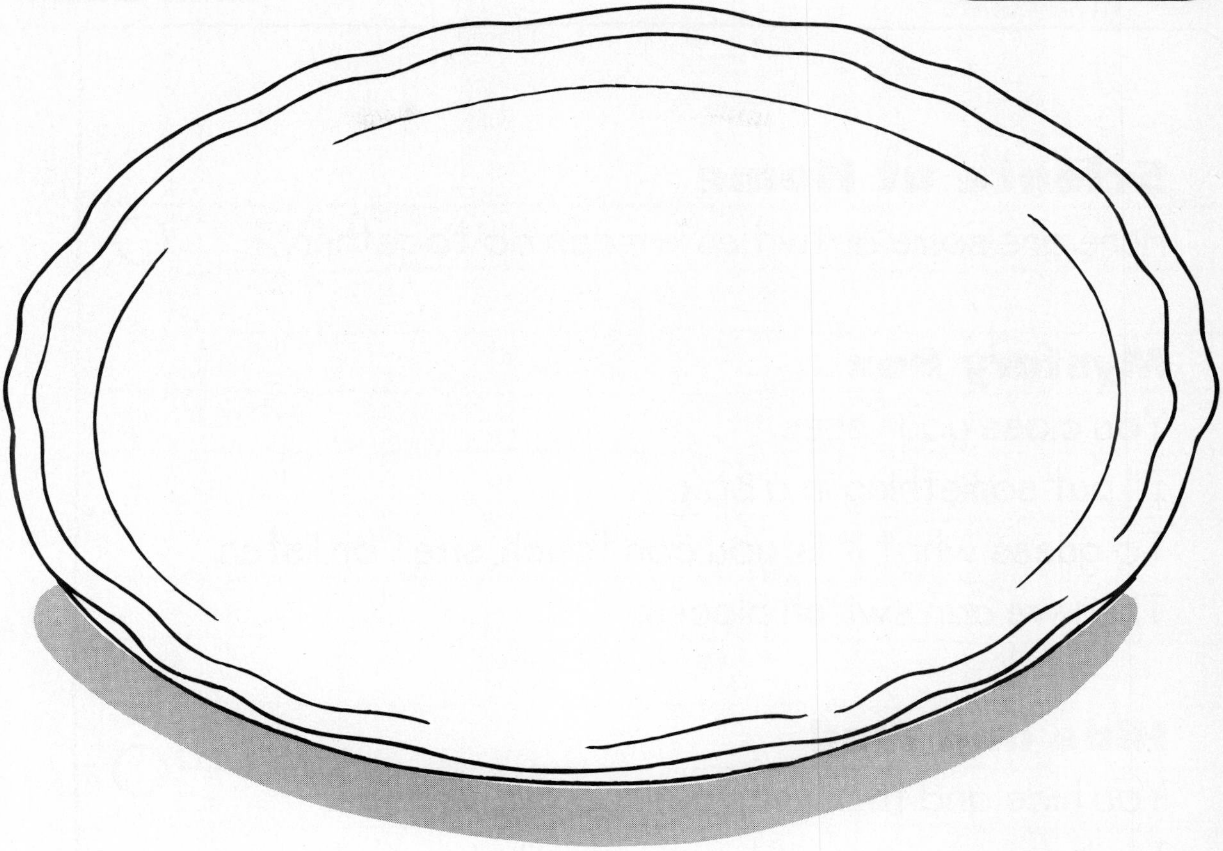

Family Activity
Unit D Chapter 1

Dear Family,
Our class will be learning about the senses. We will use our senses to describe objects. In the space, I drew a picture of my favorite food. I can tell how it looks, tastes, smells, sounds, and feels when I eat it. The other side of this letter has ideas for things that you and I can do together to find out more about the senses.

Name ____________________

Family Activity
Unit D Chapter 1

Science at Home

Here are some activities we can do together.

Mystery Box

You close your eyes.
I'll put something in a box.
To guess what it is, you can touch, smell, or listen.
Then we can switch places.

Hide and Find

You hide and then keep whispering my name.
I will use my sense of hearing to find you.
Then we'll switch—I will hide and you will find me.

Science in the Community

Take a "my senses" walk with your child in your neighborhood. While walking, encourage your child to describe what he or she sees, hears, smells, and touches. After your walk, encourage your child to draw pictures about your community.

Name ____________________

Ways of Seeing

Draw.

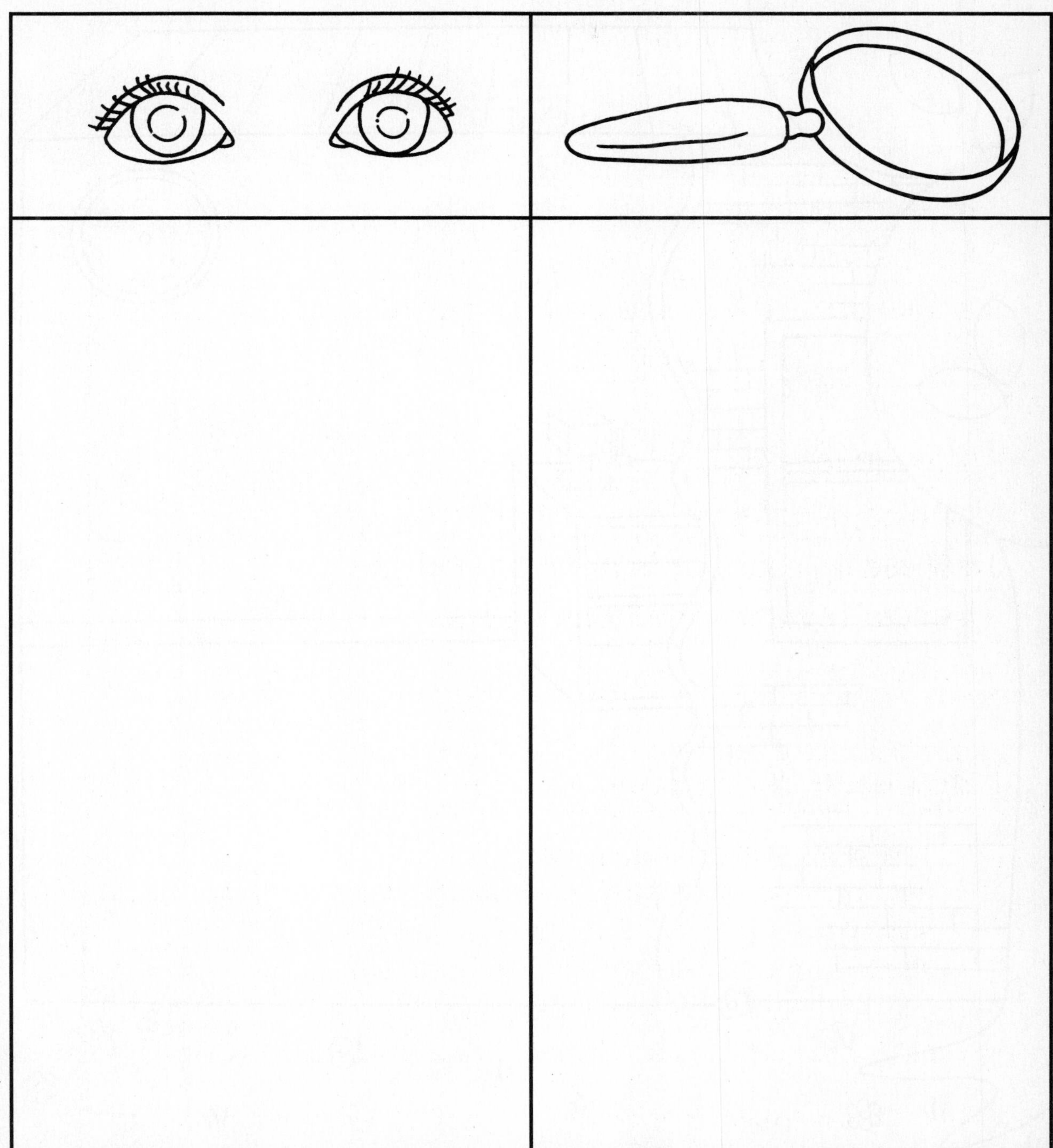

Notes for Home Your child drew pictures to show how an object looks with his or her eyes and then with a hand lens.
Home Activity: Have your child choose an object and describe its color, shape, and size.

Name ______________________________

Sounds Around Us

Listen, then draw.

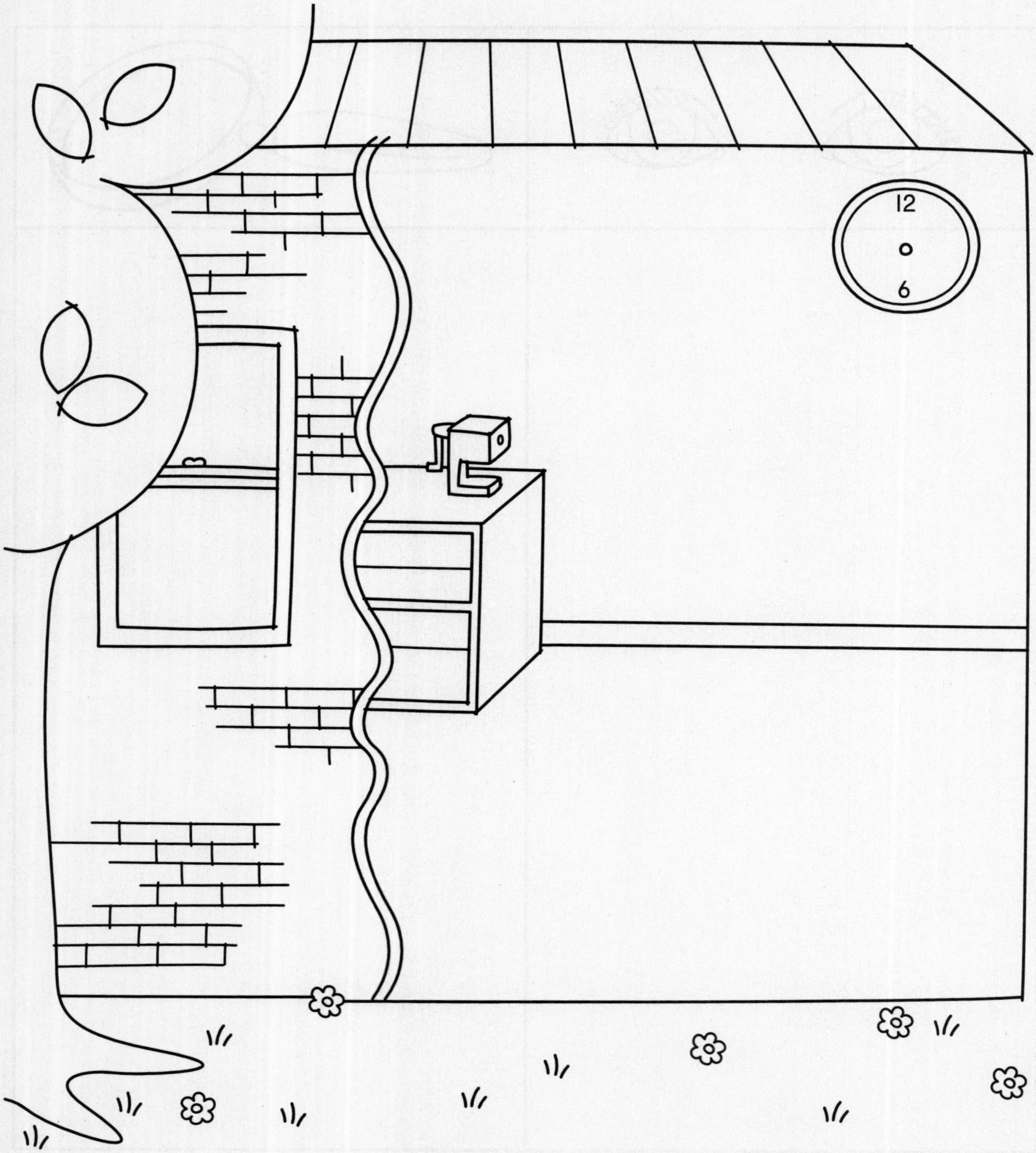

Notes for Home Your child drew pictures of things making sounds heard inside and outside our classroom.
Home Activity: Have your child look around your home and identify objects that make loud, soft, high, or low sounds.

Name ______________________________

Explore the sense of sight.

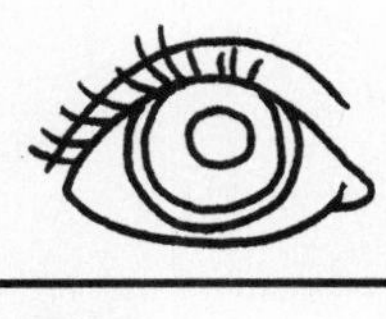
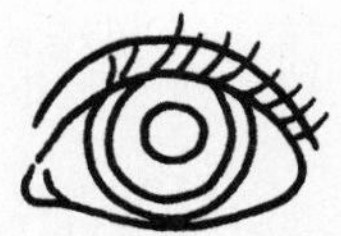
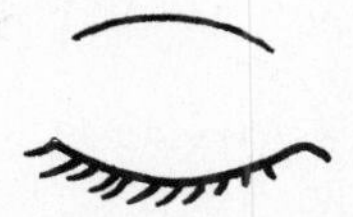
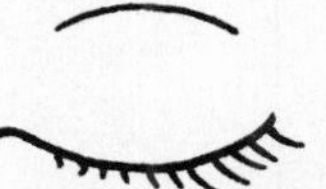

Predict.	Predict.

Record.	Record.

Notes for Home Your child predicted and recorded where the bean bag landed after each toss. ***Home Activity:*** Play a game such as "Pin the Tail on the Donkey" with your child and talk about the importance of eye sight.

Name ______________________________________

What a Smell!

Notes for Home Your child colored things that have pleasant odors and crossed out things that have unpleasant odors.
Home Activity: Have your child name several things that have a pleasant odor.

Name ___________________________

Snack Food Tastes

Draw.

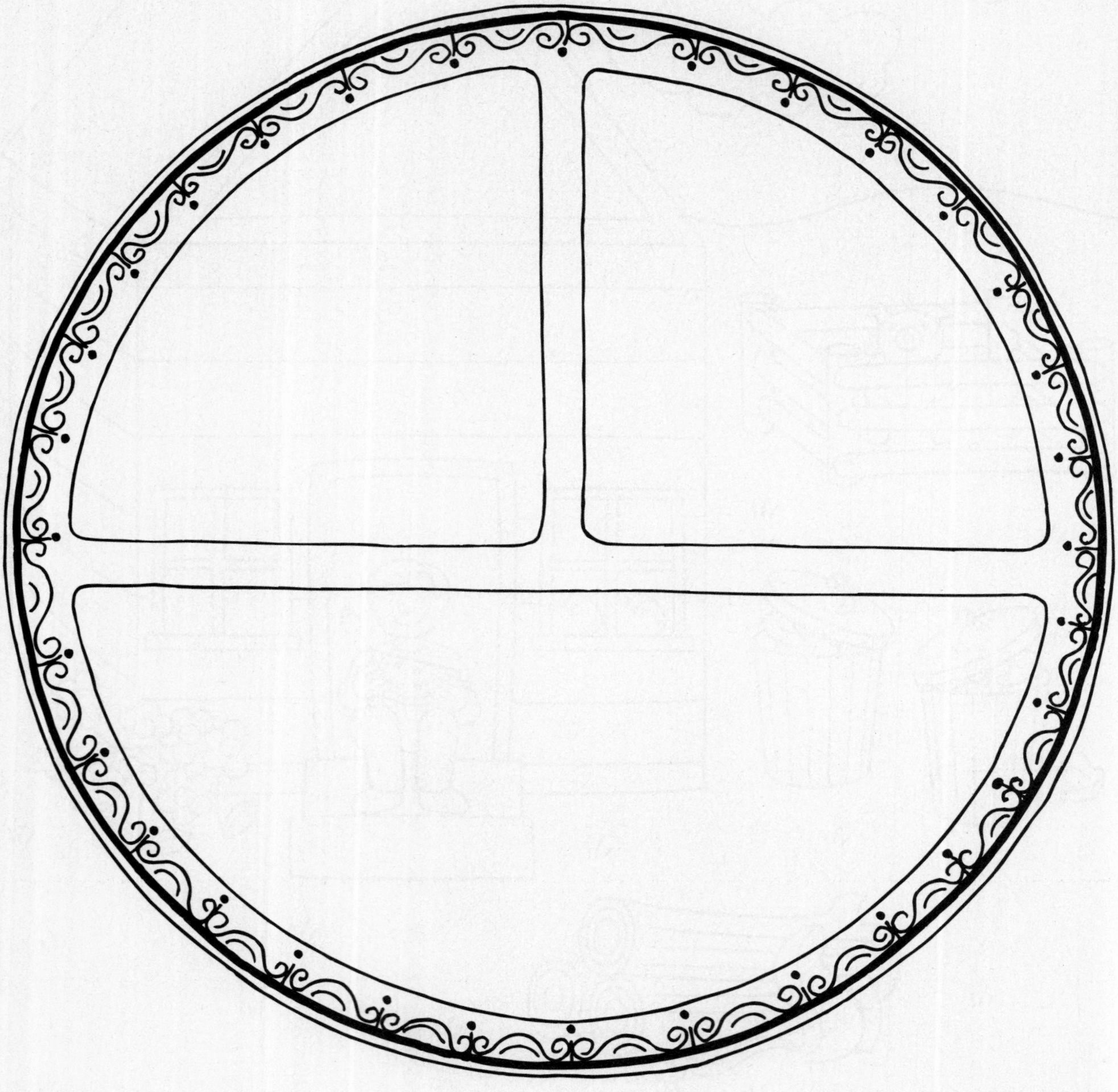

Notes for Home Your child drew or cut and pasted pictures of snacks with different tastes.
Home Activity: Ask your child to name foods that are family favorites. Help your child use words such as *sweet*, *sour*, *salty*, or *spicy* to describe the taste of each food.

Name ______________________________

Explore apples.

Draw.

Write.

Notes for Home Your child wrote or dictated words to show how he or she can use the senses to gather information about an apple.
Home Activity: The next time you and your child eat a vegetable, such as a carrot or green pepper, help your child use his or her senses to explore and talk about the vegetable.

Name ______________________

Feeling a Mystery Object

Draw what you felt.

Write about it.

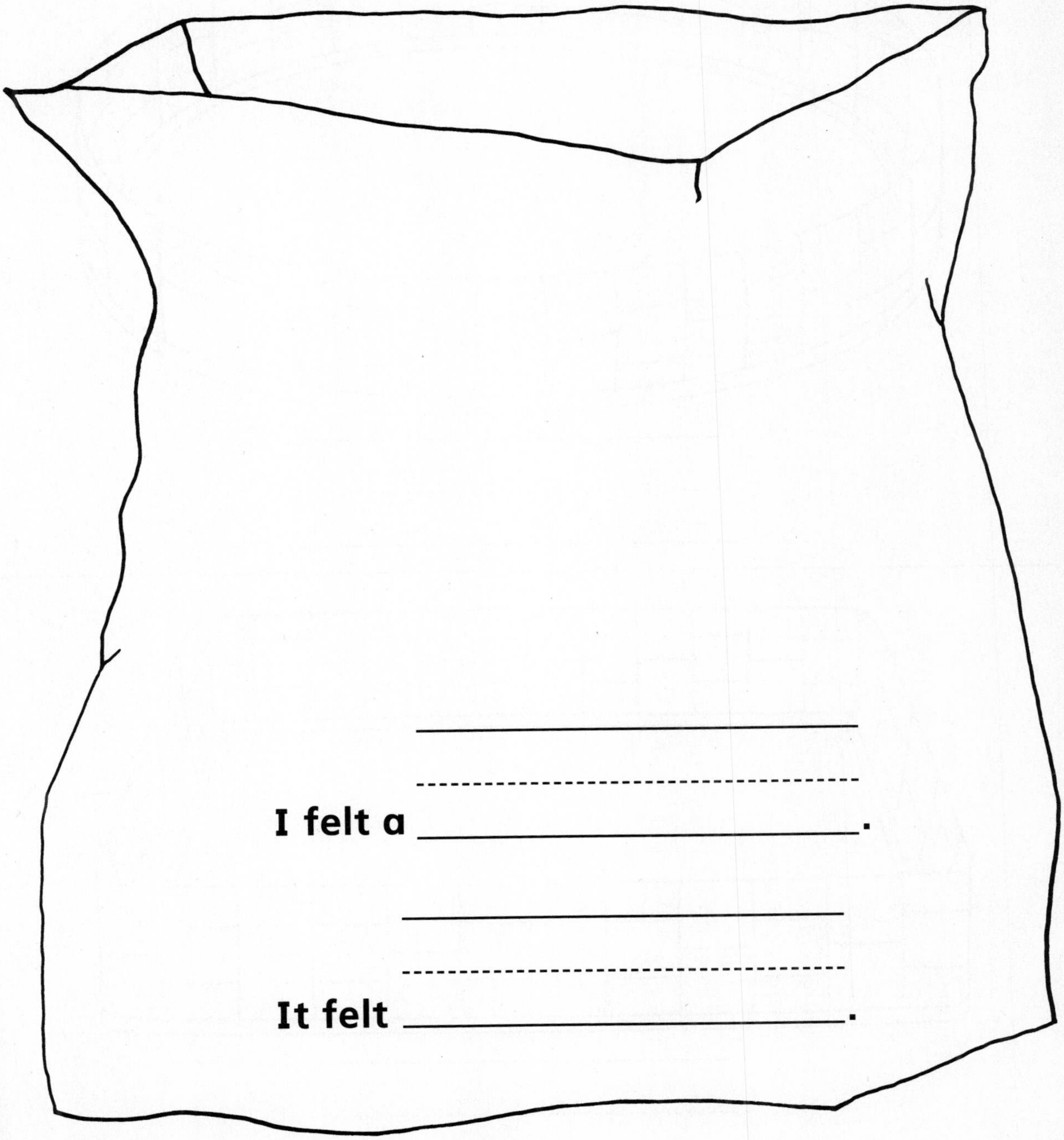

I felt a ______________________.

It felt ______________________.

Notes for Home Your child used the sense of touch to identify a mystery object.
Home Activity: Place one small object with a distinct texture in a pillowcase and ask your child to describe and then identify the object using only the sense of touch.

Name ______________________________

Sorting by Texture

Draw your groups.

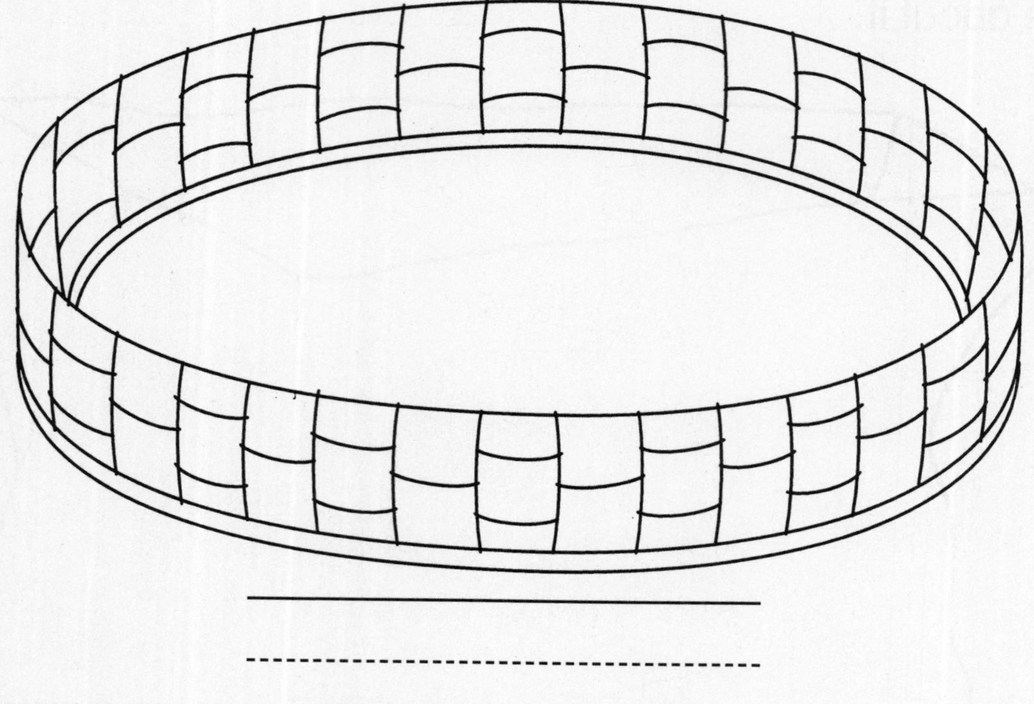

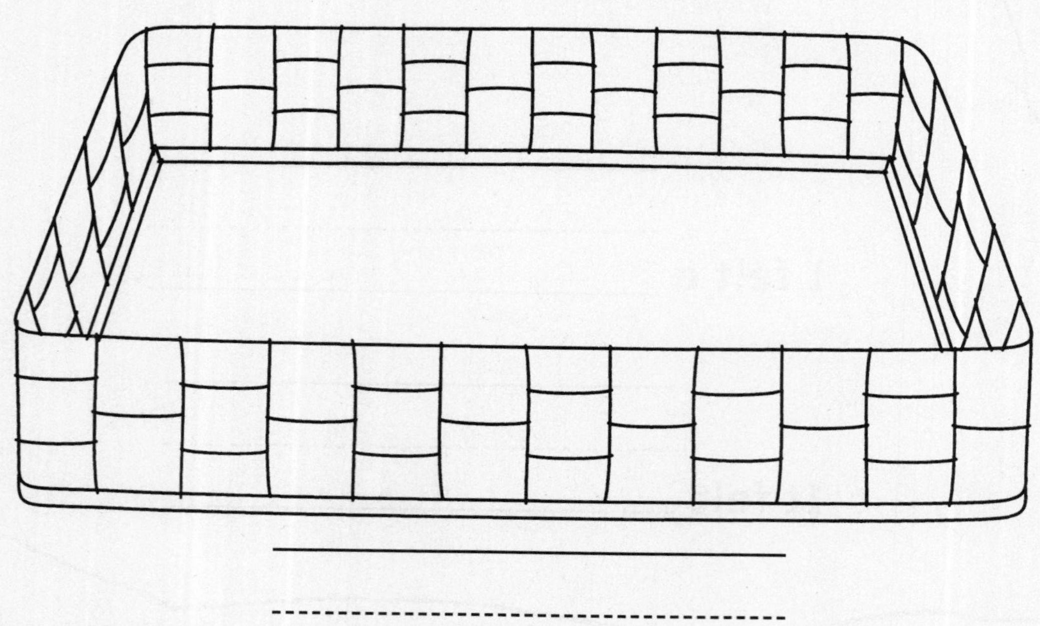

Notes for Home Your child drew two groups of objects sorted by texture.
Home Activity: When you are folding laundry, invite your child to sort the items by texture. Talk about how each item feels.

Name ______________________________

Explore textures.

Draw.

Soft	
Smooth	
Rough	
Hard	

Notes for Home Your child matched objects with like textures by drawing what was in the bag and by drawing another object with like texture.
Home Activity: Help your child find something smooth and something rough. Touch each object and talk about how they feel different.

Name ______________________________

1 + 1 = 2

Dear Family,

Our class will be learning about some parts of the body and how we use these parts. We will also find out more about how people grow and change and ways people are alike and different. In the space, I drew a picture of something I can do now that I couldn't do a year ago. The other side of this letter has ideas for things that you and I can do together to find out more about ways people grow and change over time.

Name ______________________________

Family Activity
Unit D Chapter 2

Science at Home

Here are some activities we can do together.

Look at Me Grow

We can look at some photos of me.
You can tell me how old I was.
I can put the photos in order.
We can talk about how I've grown!

I Can Do It!

I can do many new things.
I'll act one out for you to guess.
I'll tell you how I learned to do it.
Then I'll share something I want to learn to do.

Science in the Community

As you're out and about in your neighborhood, play an "I Spy" game with your child in which you look for people at different stages of life. Talk with your child about ways that people are alike and different.

Name ____________________

Explore Activity
Unit D Chapter 2

A Puppet Like Me

Draw.

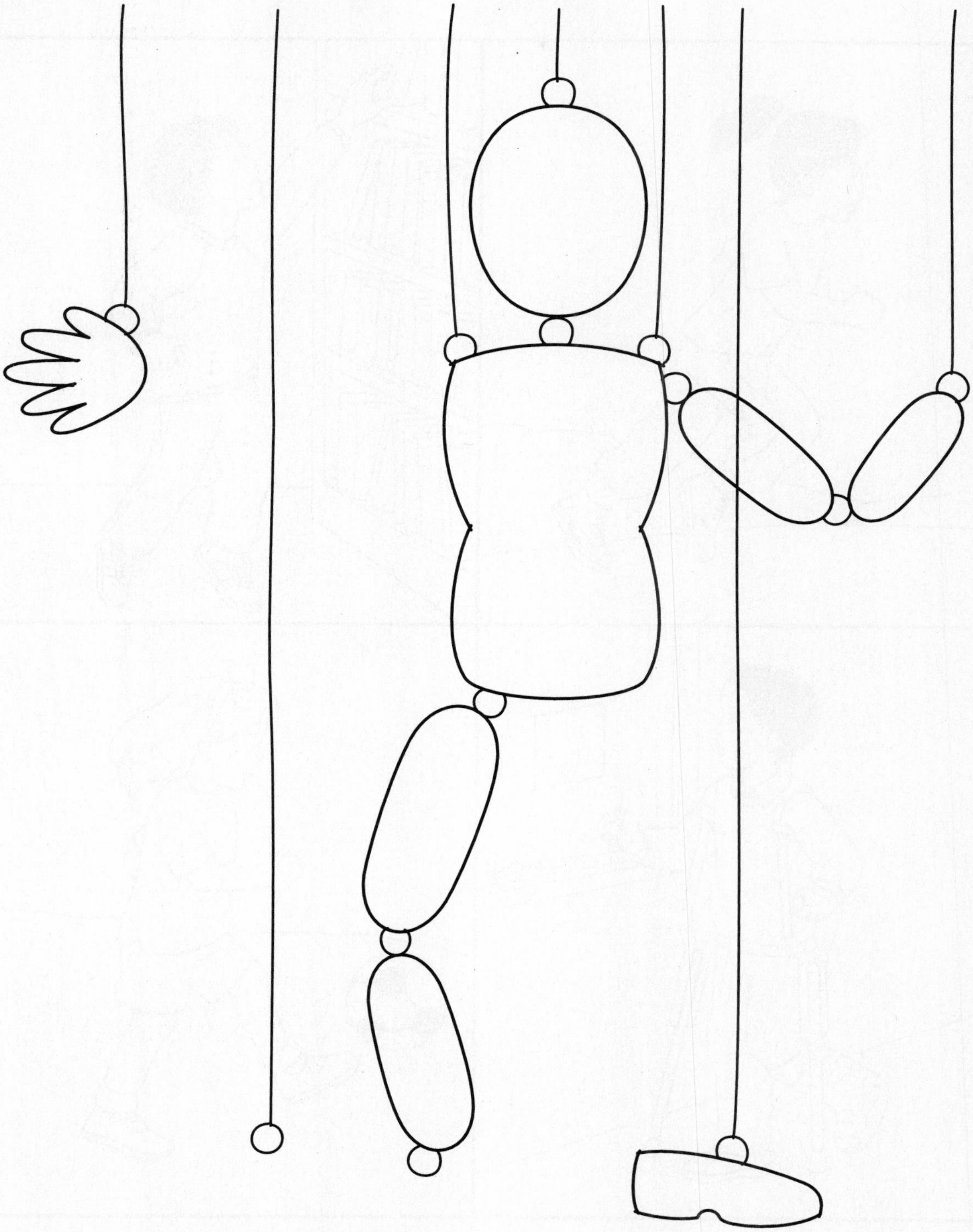

Notes for Home Your child drew missing parts to complete a puppet.
Home Activity: Play a game such as "Simon Says" in which you name different parts of the body for your child to identify.

Name ______________________________

Using Your Body

Circle.

Notes for Home Your child identified which parts of the body are used in certain activities.
Home Activity: Invite your child to tell you what body parts he or she uses when picking up toys, making a bed, or sweeping the floor.

Name ____________________

Explore Activity
Unit D Chapter 2

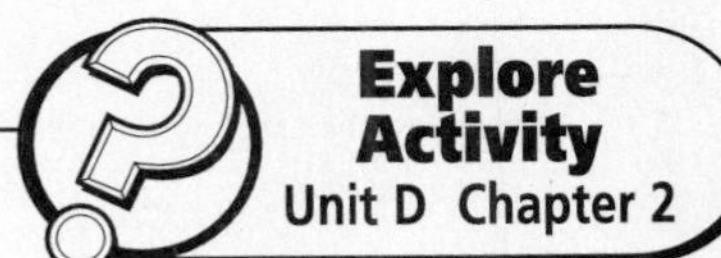

Explore balance and body parts.

Circle.

Underline.

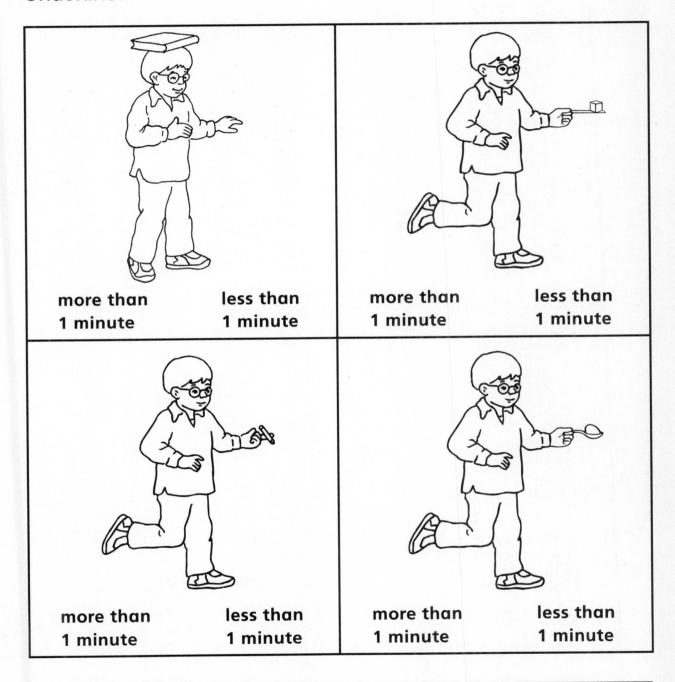

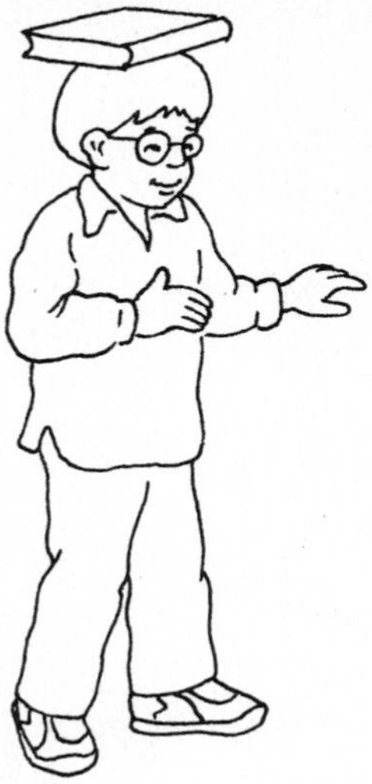

more than 1 minute **less than 1 minute**

more than 1 minute **less than 1 minute**

more than 1 minute **less than 1 minute**

more than 1 minute **less than 1 minute**

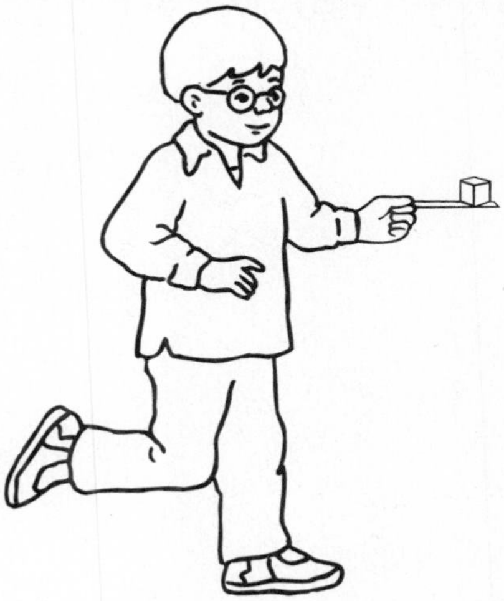

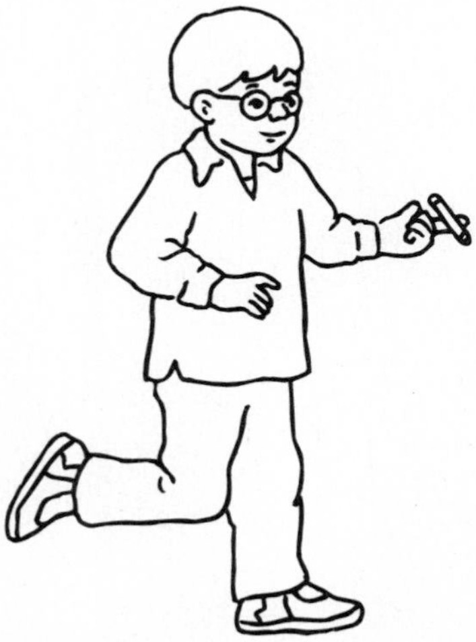

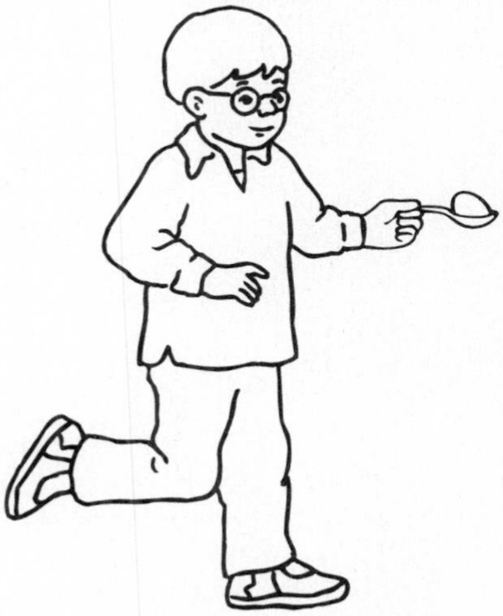

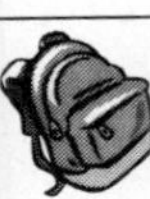

Notes for Home Your child explored balancing for one minute using different body parts. Your child circled each prediction and underlined each result.
Home Activity: With your child, try balancing a book on your heads and walking the length of a hallway. Talk about what parts of the body had to work together to balance the book.

Name ______________________________

Then and Now

Draw.

Write.

Then I could ______________________.

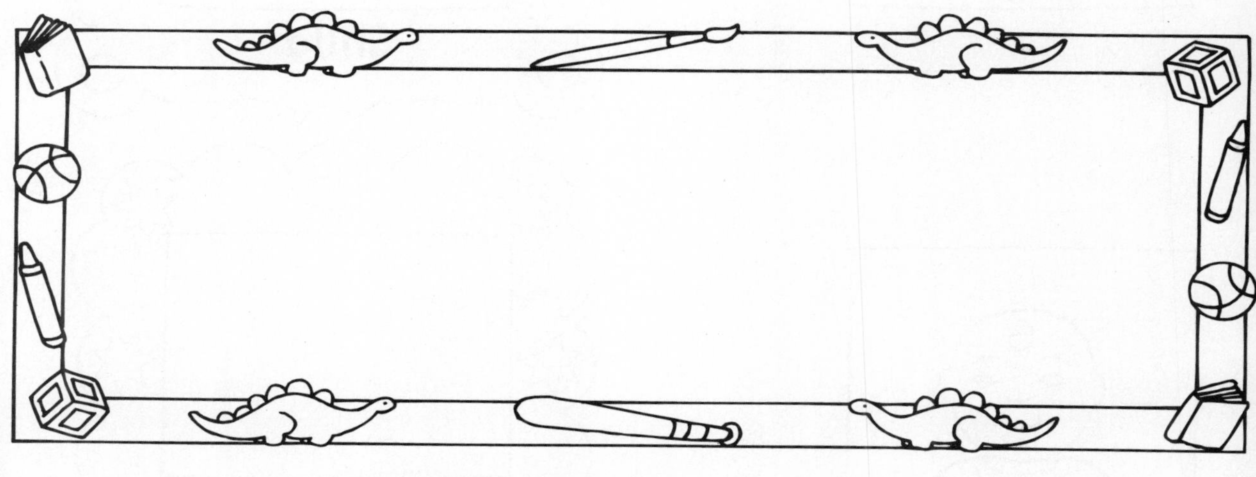

Now I can ______________________.

Notes for Home Your child drew and wrote about being a baby and being himself or herself now. ***Home Activity:*** Invite your child to talk with you about something that he or she would like to be able to do next year.

Name ______________________________

Growing Up

Order.

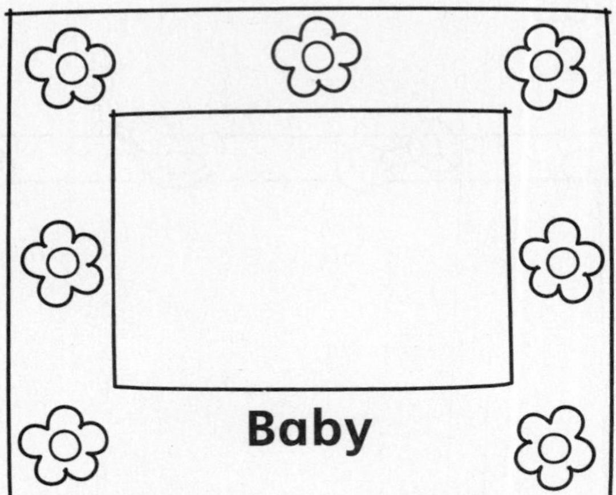

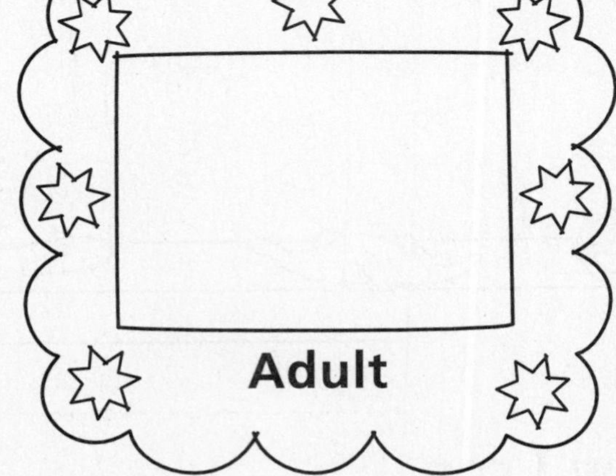

Notes for Home Your child identified the three stages of life by drawing lines to show which picture should be in which picture frame.
Home Activity: If possible, look at family pictures with your child and talk about the three stages of life: baby, child, and adult.

Name ____________________

Explore teeth.

Color.

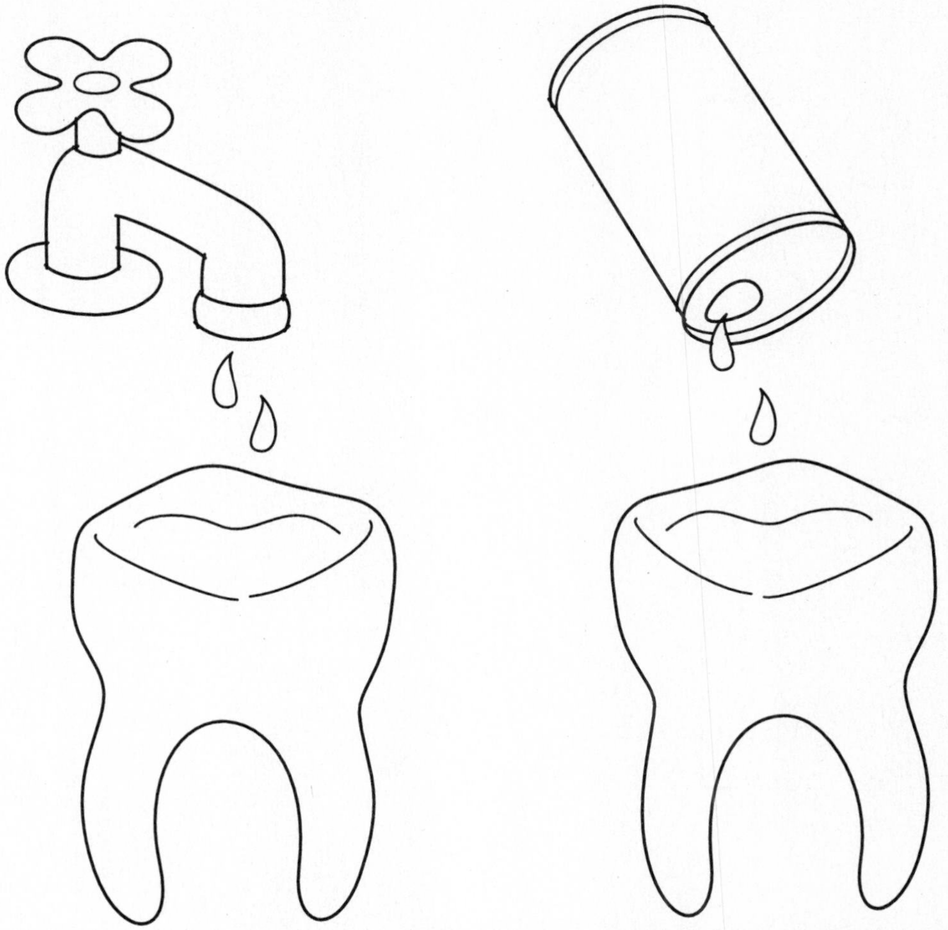

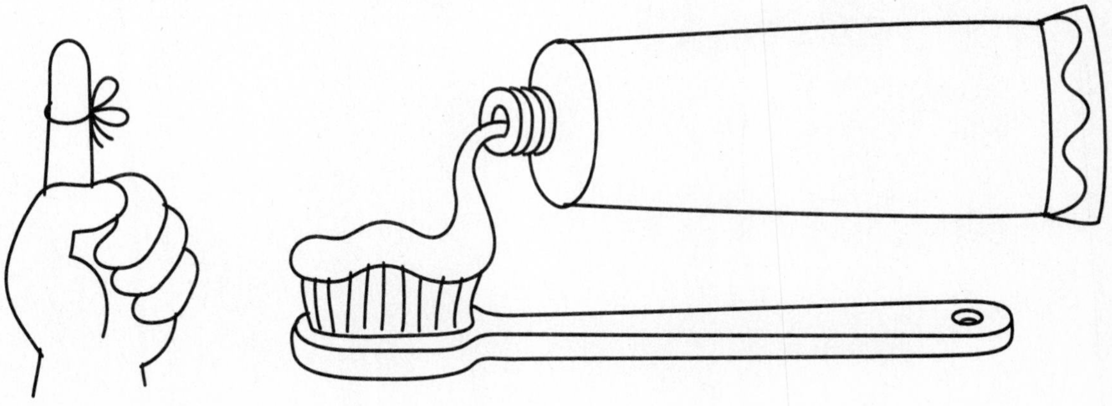

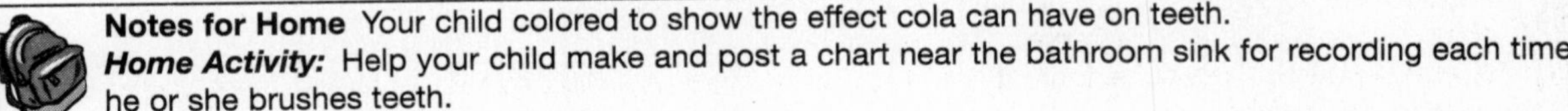

Notes for Home Your child colored to show the effect cola can have on teeth.
Home Activity: Help your child make and post a chart near the bathroom sink for recording each time he or she brushes teeth.

Name ____________________

Explore Activity
Unit D Chapter 2

Lend a Hand

Press.

Notes for Home Your child compared the size of his or her hand with that of a friend.
Home Activity: Have your child place the palm of his or her hand against yours. How are your hands alike? How are they different?

Name ______________________________

What I Like to Do

Draw.

Write.

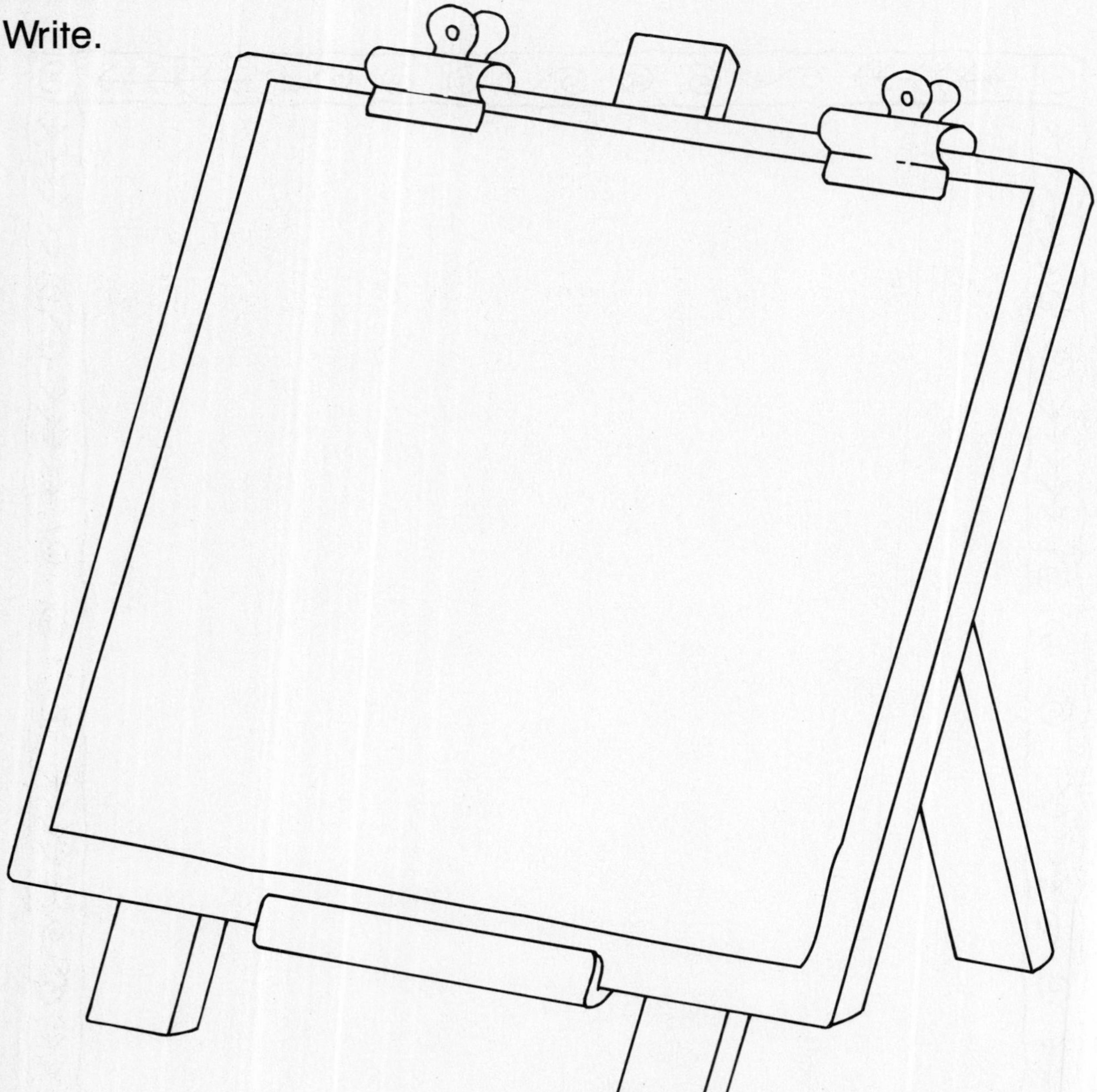

I like to ______________________.

Notes for Home Your child drew and wrote about a special interest.
Home Activity: Talk about something that you enjoyed doing as a child. If possible, you and your child might have fun doing this activity together.

Name ______________________________

Explore Activity
Unit D Chapter 2

Explore fingerprints.

Press.

Notes for Home Your child made his or her fingerprints, then used a hand lens to observe the pattern in the fingerprints.
Home Activity: Examine your fingerprints with your child by shining a bright flashlight on your finger tips. Talk about the patterns.

Name ____________________

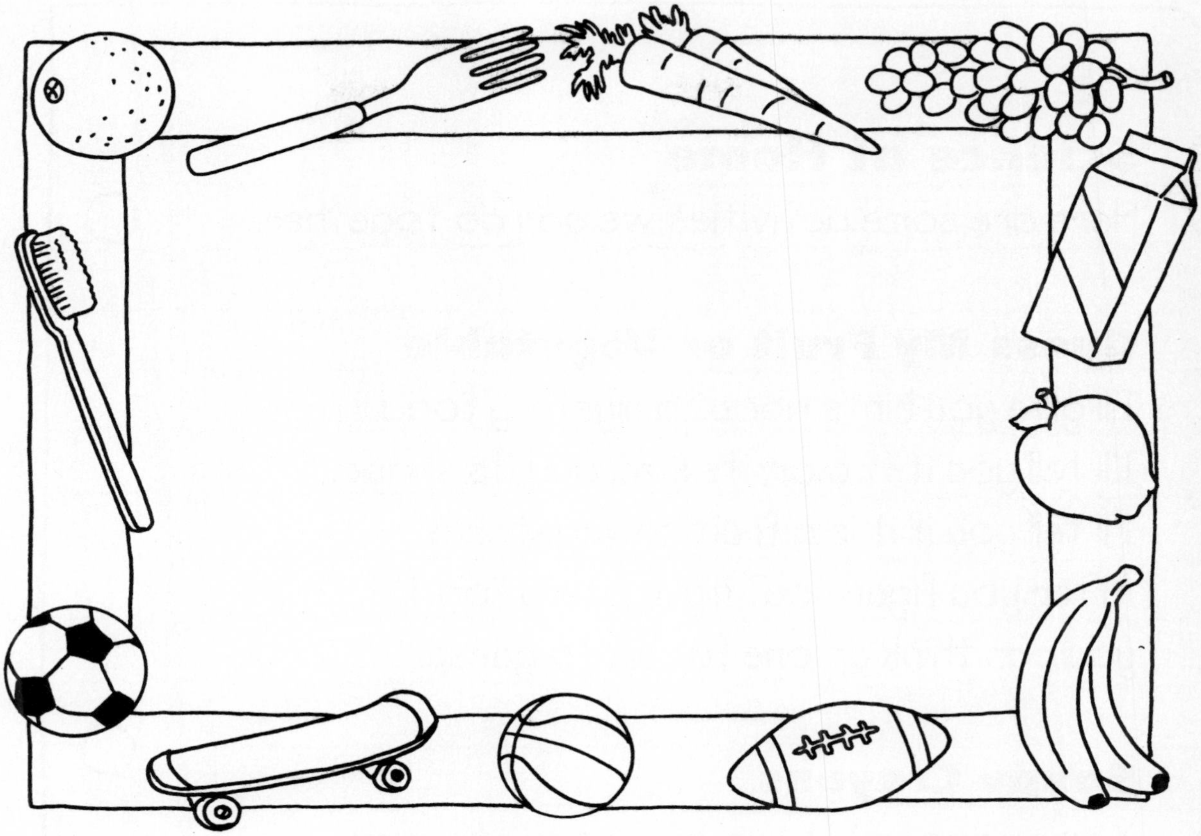

Family Activity
Unit D Chapter 3

Dear Family,

Our class will learn about things we can do to stay healthy. We will explore ways to keep fit by exercising and resting. We will also talk about foods we need to grow and stay healthy. In the space, I drew a picture of something I do to stay healthy. The other side of this letter has ideas for things you and I can do together to find out more about staying healthy.

Name ______________________________

Family Activity
Unit D Chapter 3

Science at Home

Here are some activities we can do together.

Guess My Fruit or Vegetable

I'll give you hints about a mystery food.
I'll tell you its color, its size, and its shape.
I'll tell you if it is a fruit or vegetable.
After you figure out my mystery food,
you can think up one for me to guess.

Soapy Crayons

You can pour 1/8 cup of water into a cup.
Then I will fill the cup with soap flakes
(be sure they are flakes).
After mixing it up, I will add food coloring.
We can spoon the mixture into an ice cube tray.
We'll let the cubes dry for one or two days.
Then I can use the soap crayons in the tub!

Science in the Community

The next time the two of you grocery shop, spend time in the produce section. What fruits and vegetables can your child identify? Are there new ones the two of you would like to try? Talk about why hand washing is important before preparing or eating any food.

Name ____________________

Explore Activity
Unit D Chapter 3

Ways to Exercise

Draw.

Write.

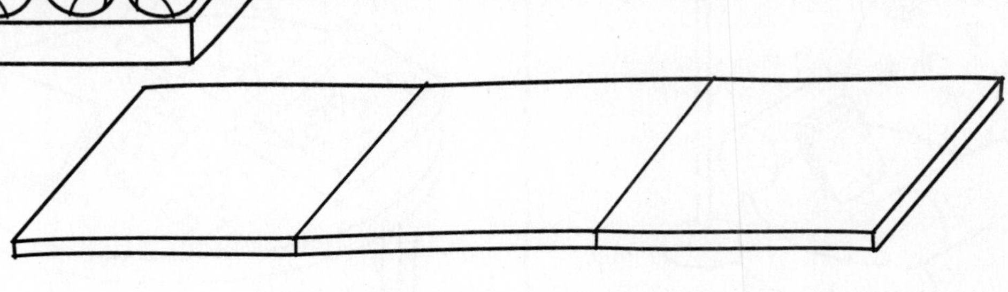

____

I like to ____________________.

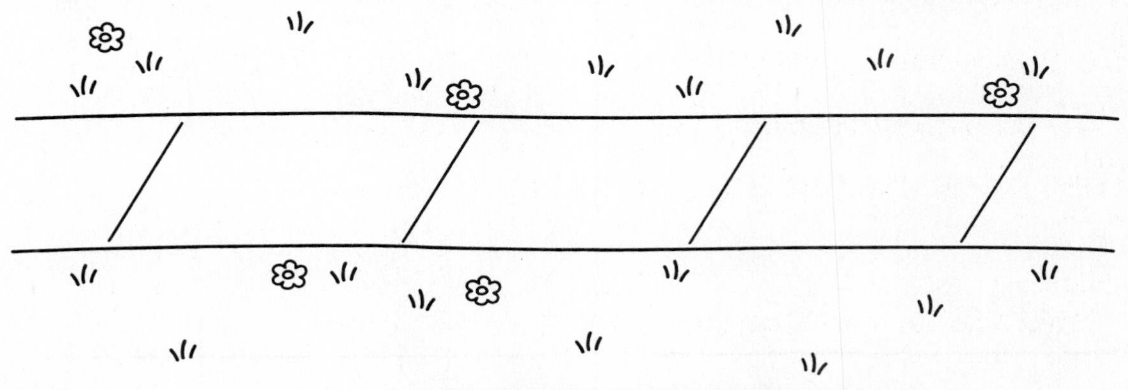

____

I like to ____________________.

Notes for Home Your child drew and wrote about favorite ways to exercise indoors and outdoors.
Home Activity: Have your child keep an exercise log for a week by drawing pictures showing how he or she exercised.

Name ______________________________

Ways to Rest

Draw.

Write.

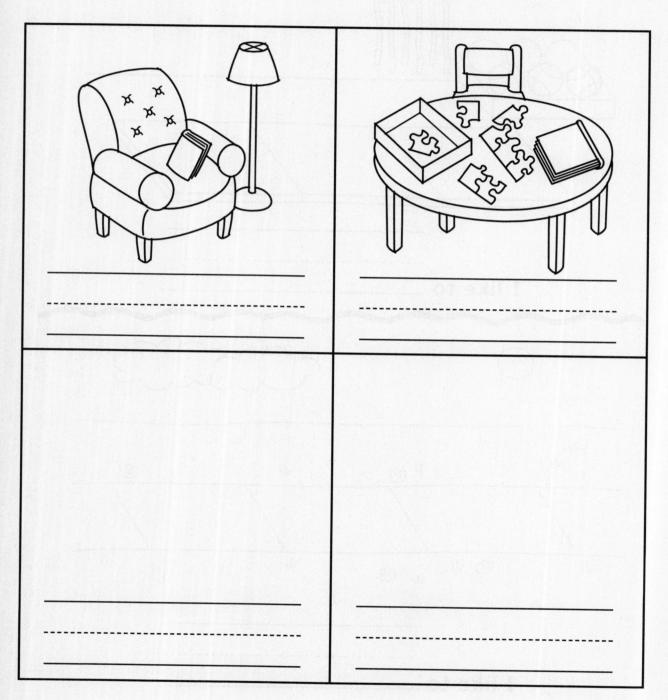

Notes for Home Your child drew ways to rest.

Home Activity: Invite your child to tell you why it is important to get a good night's sleep. Talk about things that help your child fall asleep.

Name ______________________________

Explore Activity
Unit D Chapter 3

Explore heartbeat.

Draw.

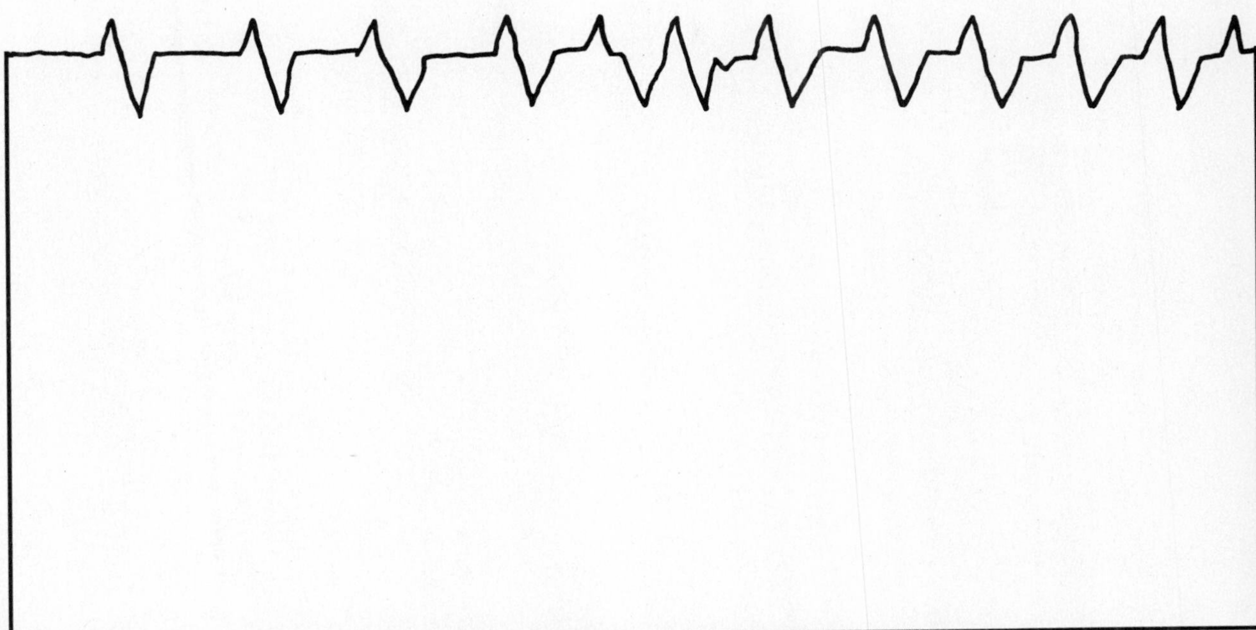

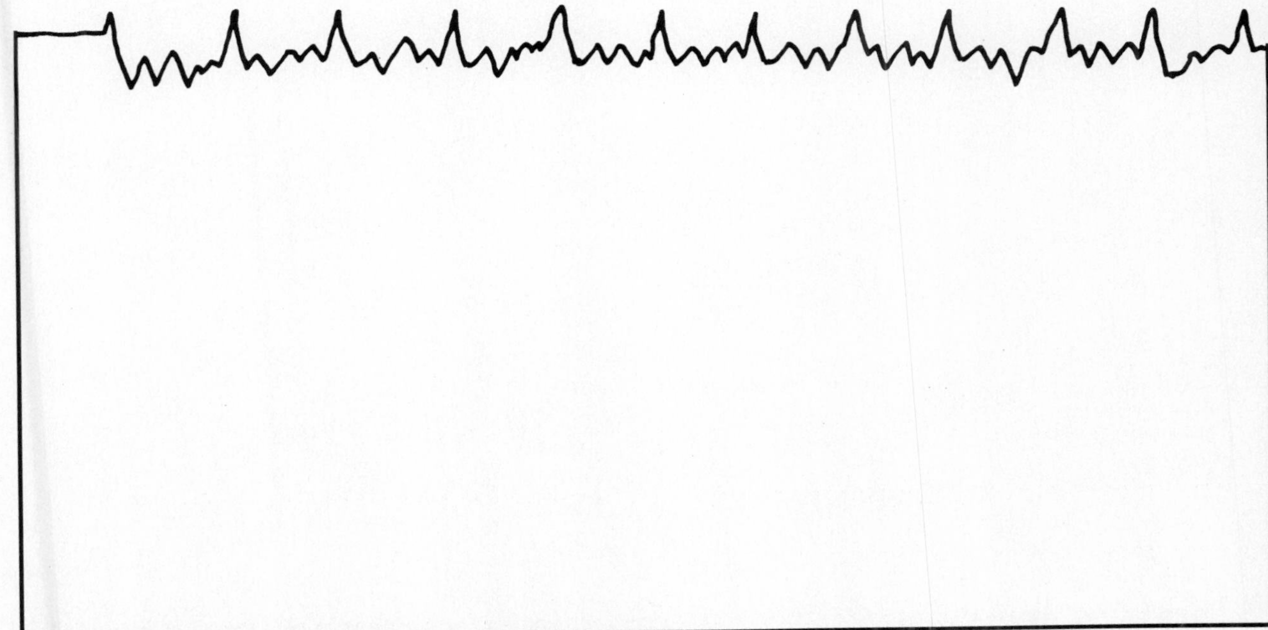

Notes for Home Your child drew pictures to show how different activities affect the heartbeat.
Home Activity: Take a brisk walk with your child around your neighborhood. As you walk, encourage your child to notice changes in his or her heartbeat and to look for other activities people do that might affect their heartbeats.

Name ______________________

Explore Activity
Unit D Chapter 3

What's for Lunch?

Color.

Fruits

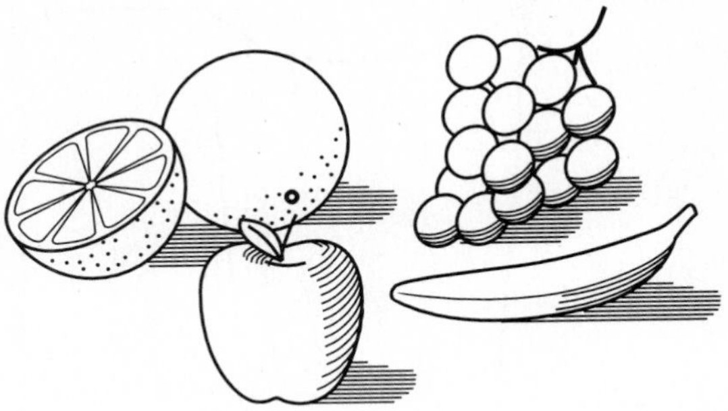

Vegetables

Draw.

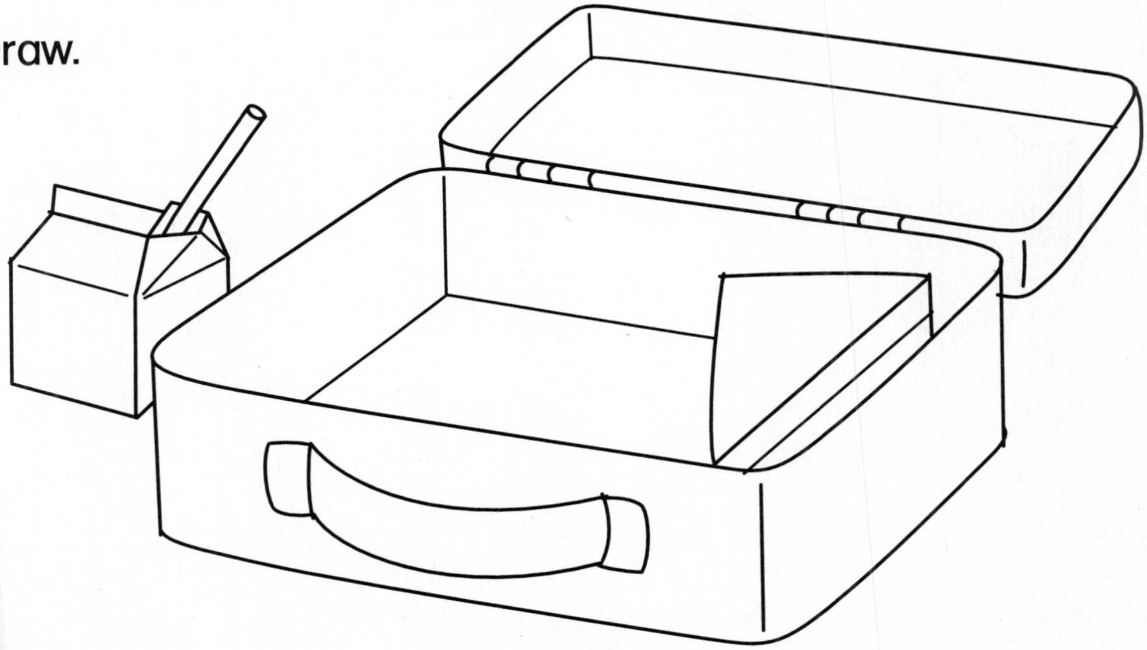

I like ______________ and ______________ for lunch.

Notes for Home Your child colored fruits and vegetables, then drew one of each to complete a lunch. ***Home Activity:*** Invite your child to tell what he or she likes to eat for lunch on a school day. Does this lunch include at least one serving of a fruit or a vegetable?

Name ______________________________

Planning a Meal

Draw.

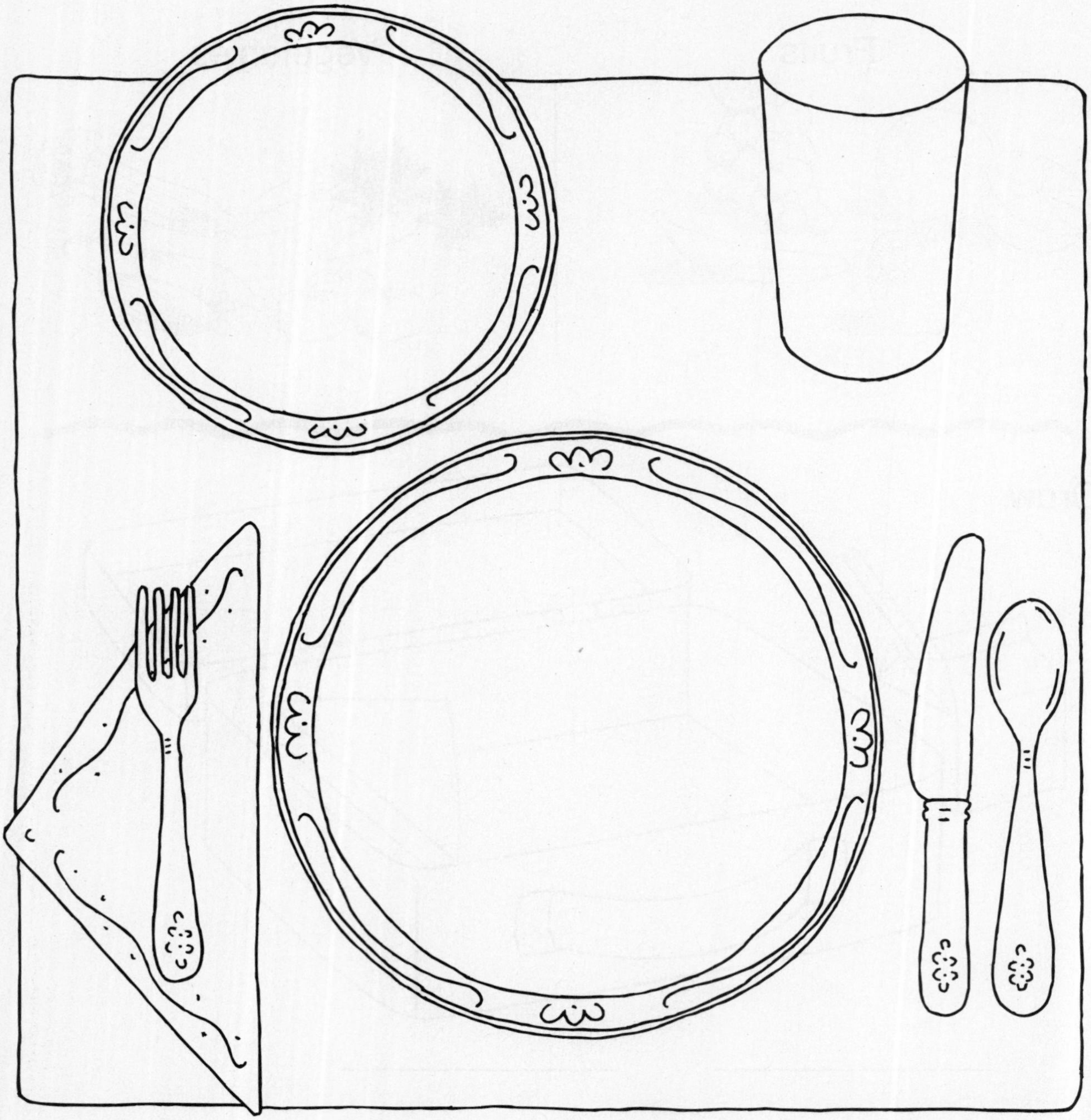

Notes for Home Your child drew foods to show a balanced meal made up of foods from at least three food groups.

Home Activity: At your next family meal, invite your child to identify several foods and tell in which food group each belongs.

Name ______________________________

Explore healthful foods.

Draw.

My Healthful Food	

Notes for Home Your child drew four characteristics of one healthful food.
Home Activity: During the week, help your child select and prepare a favorite healthful snack.

Name ______________________________

Experiment Activity
Unit D Chapter 3

Experiment with foods.

Draw.

Fat	No Fat

Notes for Home Your child tested foods and drew pictures to show which foods contain fat and which foods contain little or no fat.
Home Activity: With your child, test a favorite family snack for fat.

Name ______________________________

Explore Activity
Unit D Chapter 3

Rub and Scrub

Draw.

Number.

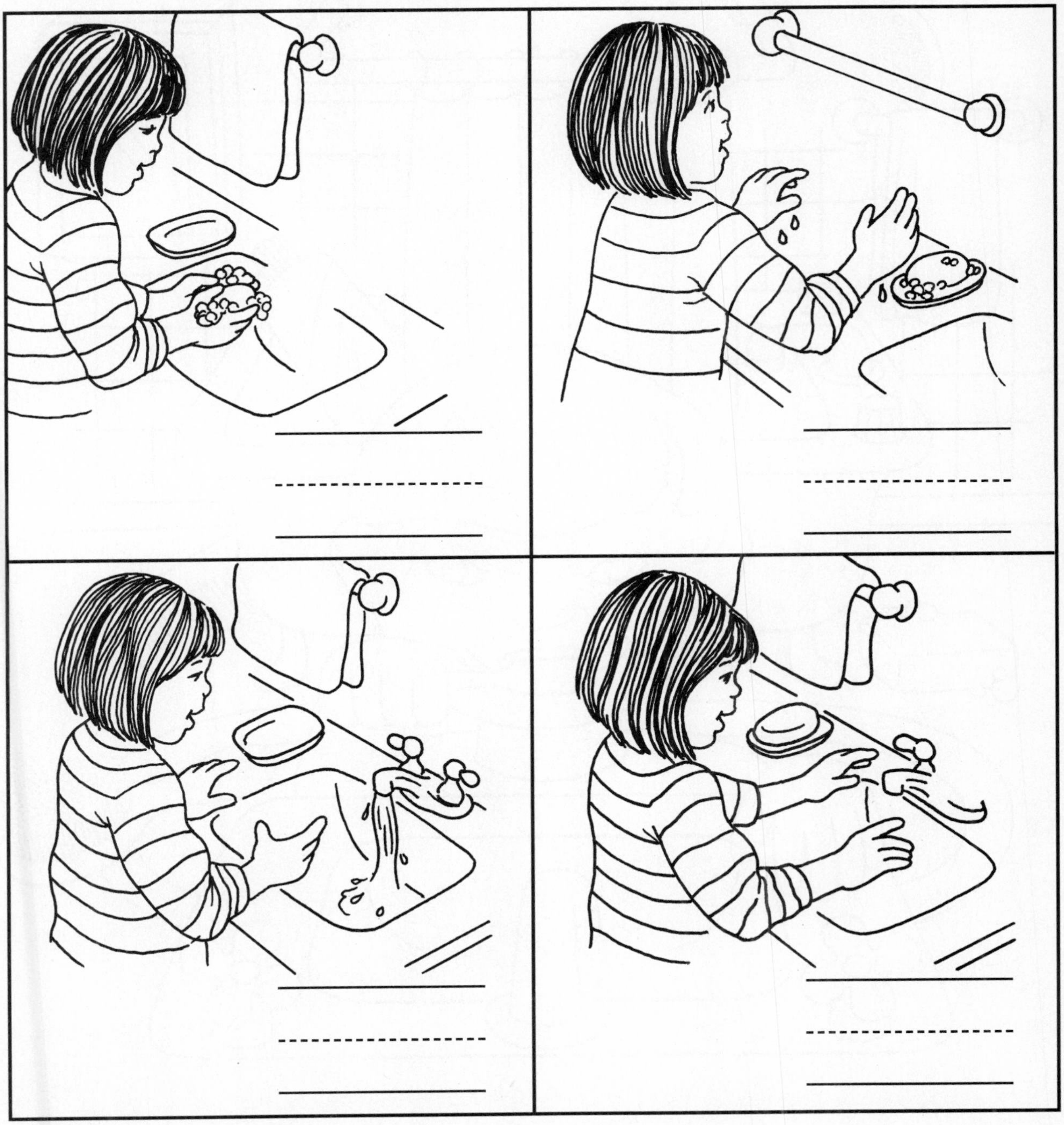

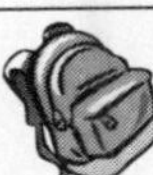

Notes for Home Your child completed and then sequenced pictures that show proper hand-washing procedures.
Home Activity: Invite your child to show you what he or she has learned about hand-washing.

Name ______________________________

Explore Activity
Unit D Chapter 3

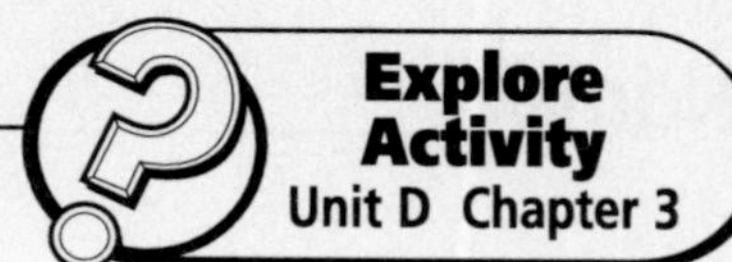

Hidden Tools

Color.

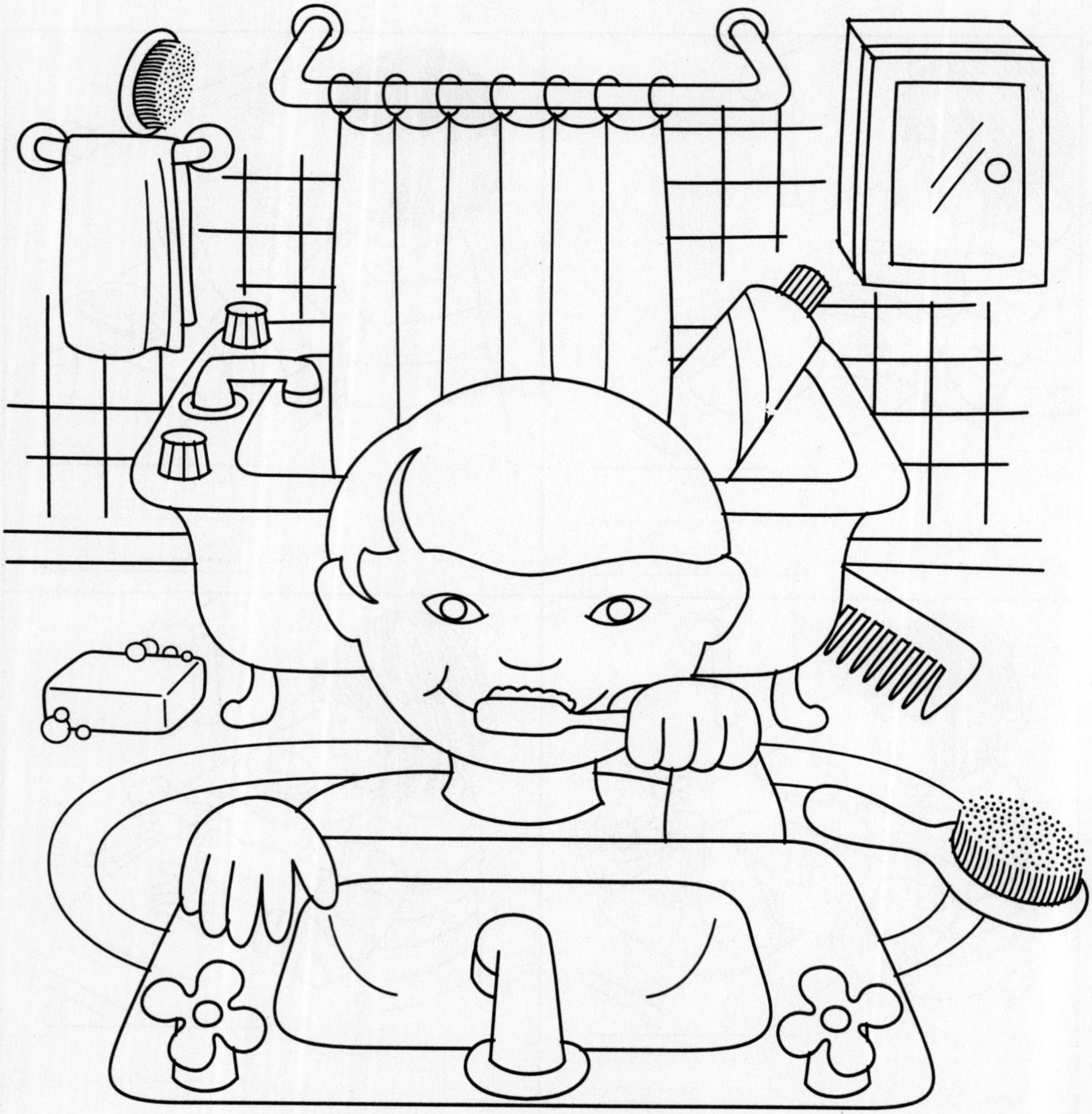

Notes for Home Your child found five hidden health care tools in the picture.
Home Activity: Have your child name each health care tool and tell how it is used to help people stay healthy.

Name ______________________________

Explore Activity
Unit D Chapter 3

Explore dirty hands.

Draw.

Touched

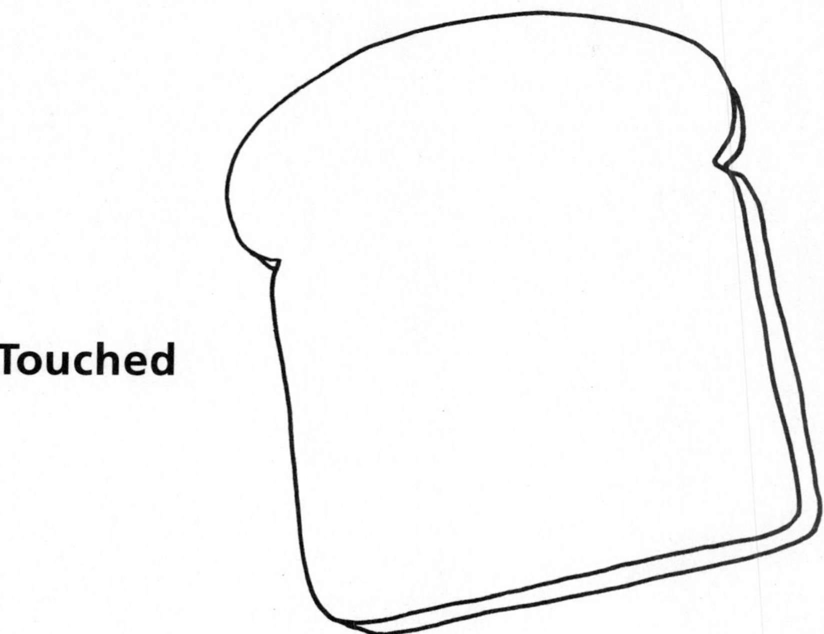

Not Touched

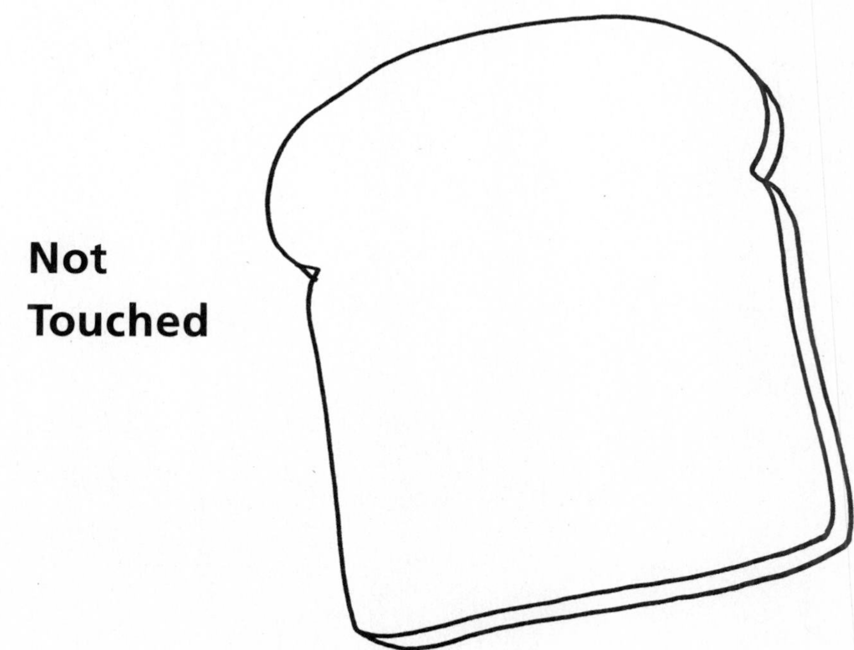

Notes for Home Your child drew pictures to show how a bread slice that was not touched by dirty hands looked and how a bread slice that was touched by dirty hands looked after several days.
Home Activity: Talk with your child about times when handwashing is important.

Name ____________________

Science Process Skill

Controlling Variables

Notes for Home Your child drew a picture of an ice cube at the beginning of a twenty-minute observation period.
Home Activity: Invite your child to describe the experiment. Ask: "Will the temperature stay the same? (yes) Will the location stay the same? (yes) Will the time stay the same? (no) What do you think will happen?"

Name ______________________________

Science Process Skill

Practice Controlling Variables

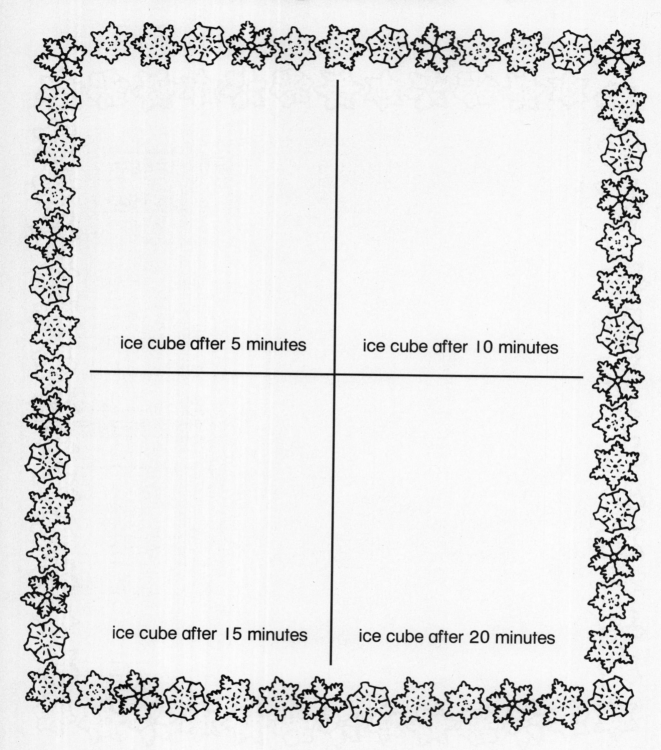

ice cube after 5 minutes	ice cube after 10 minutes
ice cube after 15 minutes	ice cube after 20 minutes

Notes for Home Your child drew pictures to show how an ice cube looks at five-minute intervals when it is at a constant temperature.
Home Activity: The next time you bake a cake with your child, point out that the temperature and location stay the same, only the time changes. Observe the cake at ten-minute intervals and talk about how the cake changes over time.

Name ____________________

Science Process Skill

Experimenting

Circle.

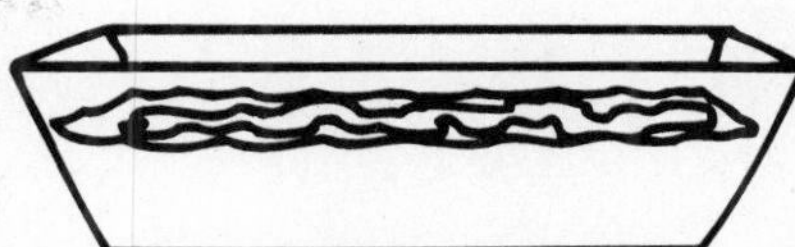

+ 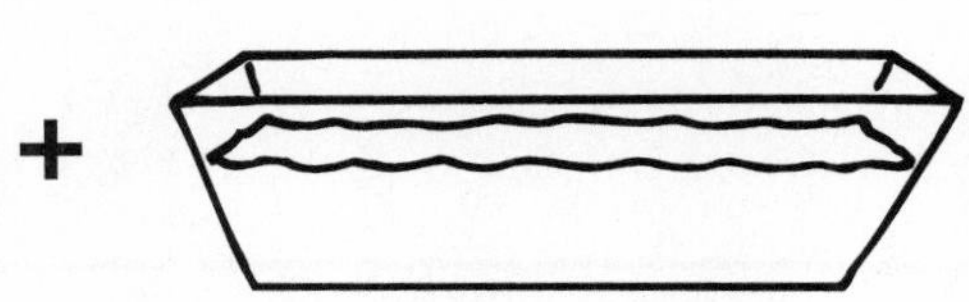 = 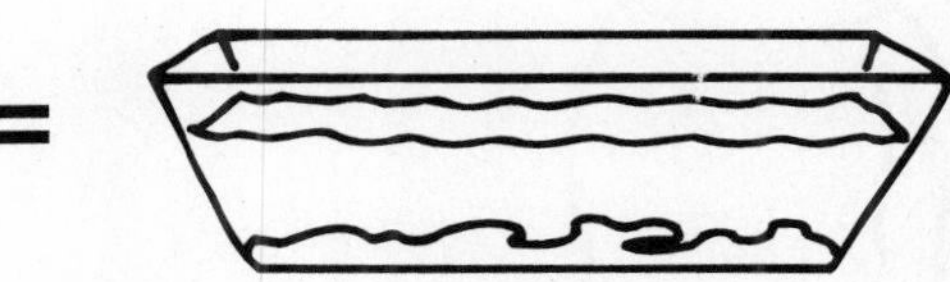

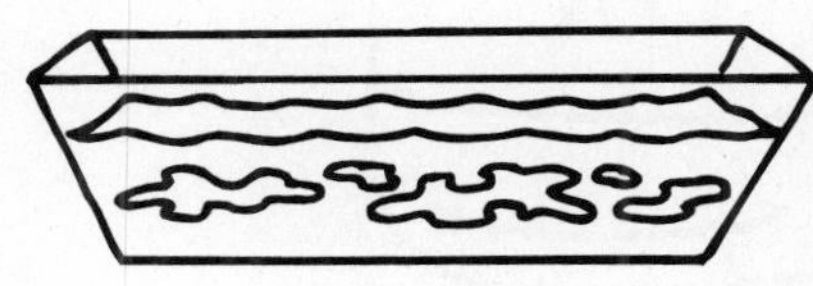

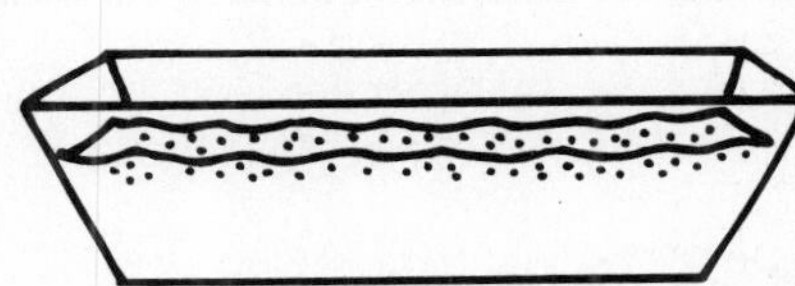

+ 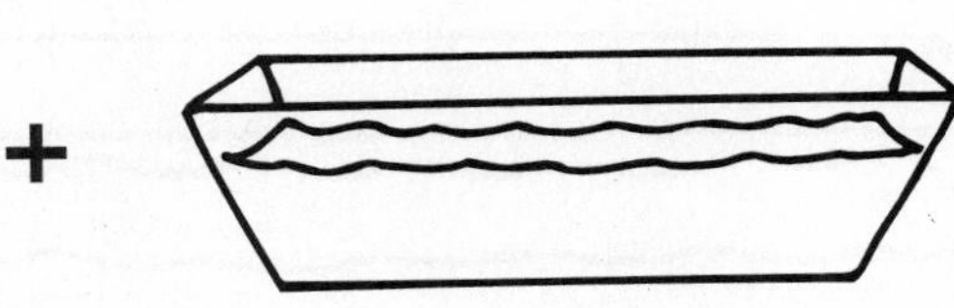 = 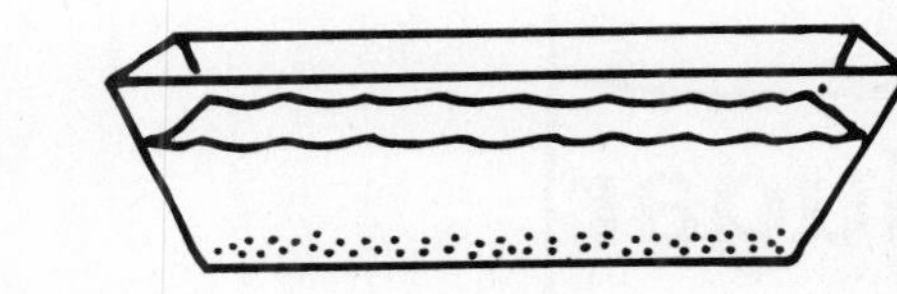

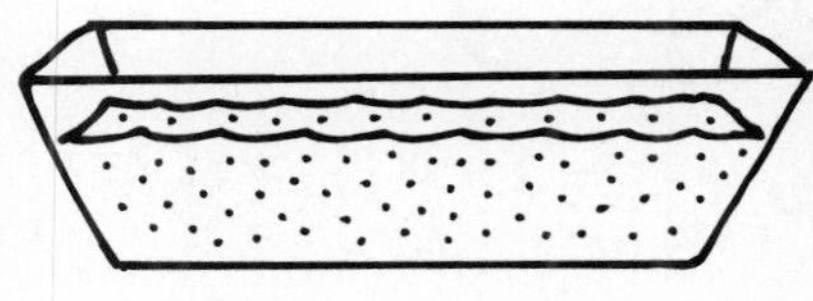

Notes for Home Your child circled pictures to show what he or she thinks will happen if oil or sugar is added to water.
Home Activity: Ask your child what he or she thinks will happen if you add one tablespoon of a liquid, such as syrup, to a cup of water. Experiment to find out.

Name ________________

Science Process Skill

Practice Experimenting

Draw.

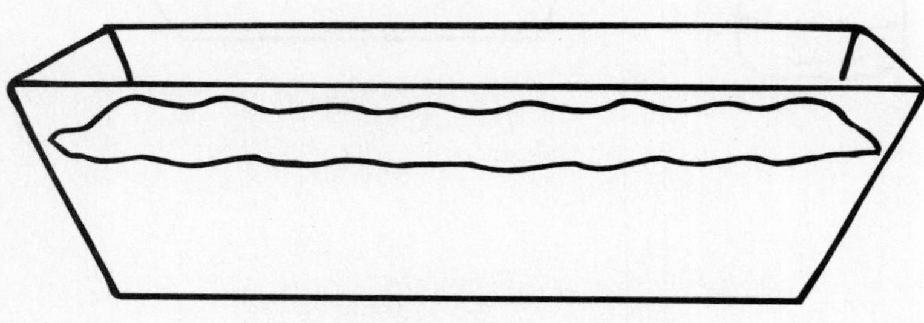

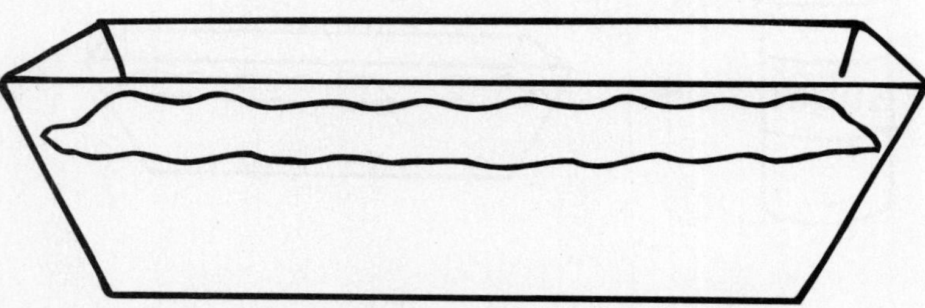

Notes for Home Your child drew pictures to show what happened when he or she added oil or sugar to water. ***Home Activity:*** Ask your child to predict what will happen if salt is added to water. Discuss why, then experiment to find out.